THIS LITTLE BLACK GIRL AIN'T
YOUR BURNT TRASH

This Little Black Girl Ain't Your Burnt Trash

by Delphina Brooks

Charleston, SC
www.PalmettoPublishing.com

This Little Black Girl Aint Your Burnt Trash
Copyright © 2022 by Delphina Brooks

First Edition

Paperback ISBN: 979-8-8229-0819-2

Contents

Introduction

A Black queen girl from the south of Florida, born in March. She never thought she would endure so much abuse, pain, make so many poor decisions, and be so lonely through it all. She always felt better days were coming when she discovered her love for GOD in her heart.

Hello. I am Delphina Brooks. My inspiration to share my story is part of my self-healing journey. It is to heal the little Black girl inside of me that was mentally, physically, emotionally, and sexually abused. She longed for approval and love from her family and a sense of belonging. This book is to tell that story.

I also hope to inspire young and older women with my story and let Black women know you are uniquely made from your hair to your feet. We are made in YHWH image. Our responsibility is to seek healing from the past pain and be an inspiration to other little Black girls, our families, and our communities. We should not look at each other as a threat. Instead, we must remove the negative stereotypes others have placed upon us.

My story is an avenue through which I heal and motivate others. These are my personal experiences, and they are not meant to bash anyone's identity. We all fall short of HIS glory, but we can always choose to be better and do better.

Revelation 1:14-15

Acknowledgments

I would like to thank GOD for His grace, mercy, favor for my life, and for always keeping me as I walked through the valley. A special thanks to my husband for being a loving person, an awesome friend, and a terrific partner who always accepts me for me.

I would like to thank my beautiful children. You endured the struggle with me, and although I did not always do things right, I always did my best. It brings me joy to see you all thrive. My stepsons as well, I thank you for helping me along the way. My strong amazing mother, I love you dearly.

My stepfather, R.I.P., I thank you for being a great father and for the awesome father/daughter memories filled with laughs.

I thank my amazing grandmother, who is also not here on Earth anymore but always here in spirit. A better day is coming for your descendants and from me sharing my story.

My late father, gone too soon, I thank you. Our last three years together, I will hold dear to my heart.

Lastly, my two beautiful granddaughters. GMA loves you; you are heaven-sent. Thank you for allowing me to be your grandmother.

Preschool

The earliest age I can remember is four years old living in Florida. I attended Turner Preschool. I was a shy preschooler who did not smile much. In my first school picture, I didn't even smile. I remember the photographer telling me to "smile!" I just hung my bottom lip down, showing all my baby teeth.

The first and only time my dad dropped me off at school was in preschool. I sat at the breakfast table that morning and did not like the mess they served at school. It smelled funny. When my dad was leaving, my teacher asked him,

"Will you be the one picking her up from school today?"

My father replied, "Yes."

She informed him that school lets out at 2:00. I sat at the table with the other children. My teacher told me I had to eat the mess on my plate. I slightly shook my head because I did not want that stinky and sticky stuff. The teacher tried to force me to eat what was apparently, "oatmeal," saying I wouldn't be able to leave the table until I ate it. Well, it was a battle between us two because I wasn't eating it. I knew about grits, but my mother never made us oatmeal.

At the end of the preschool day, all the children were getting up from our naps. I got up and noticed I had wet the cot. I immediately hid under a table. I figured the teacher wouldn't see me or realize I wet the cot.

My teacher yelled, "Delphina, you wet this cot! Where is she?"

I came from under the table, but I did not have a change of clothes, so I was left to air dry.

I had a severe problem with wetting the cot at school and the bed at home. I did not know why I had this problem or when it started. No one seemed concerned about it either. I wonder now was it before or after my older cousin molested me?

My dad did not end up picking me up from school that day. It was the first of many hurtful things to happen to that little Black girl. He also used to tell me to stop singing and that I couldn't sing. This crushed me. I loved singing and knew all the songs on the radio and all the songs on the records that my parents owned. What else am I supposed to do as a four-year-old to bring myself peace and joy?

Innocence Stolen

The first time I can recall being molested was in preschool. The perpetrator was my older cousin Demon. Sometimes my dad's mother would babysit my older brother and me. On this day, Demon and my older brother were playing in my grandmother's living room. Demon was holding me in front of him. My legs were touching the carpet, and I would swing them up, laughing, just having fun. When my legs came down, Demon would touch my private parts. I had no clue what was going on, and my older didn't know either. Looking back, he was slick with his sexual abuse.

Going to my grandmother Marcia house when it was just her was usually very fun. She would give my brother and myself money to go see the cookie lady next door. I had terrible dandruff and sores on my scalp, and no one knew the cause of this. My grandma, Marcia, tried a home remedy to cure this. She had the "magic solution" to pour bleach onto my scalp. It set my head on fire and did not eliminate the issue.

When playing with children, particular physical contact should be off-limits, involving picking children up, tickling, or piggyback rides.

My mother took me to the doctor, who prescribed me a medicated shampoo. He explained that I had ringworms. The shampoo stank, but it did get the job done. I was able to grow some beautiful and thick long hair.

Kindergarten and First Grade Nightmare

A child would think that transitioning to elementary school was supposed to be exciting. I did not attend the first week of the new school. I feared all the newness and things I would be unfamiliar with. Even riding on a public-school bus was scary, and I did not want to walk alone.

My older sibling, who is just one year older than me, Tony, told me he didn't want me walking with him to catch the bus. I didn't even know where the bus stop was. I yelled for Tony, and he waited for a little and then kept walking. I just turned around and went back home.

My mom left for work at the crack of dawn, so I stayed home the first week without her knowing. While I was at home, I would watch The Price is Right, Sesame Street, and my favorite afternoon tv show was The Banana Splits. My lunch was a bologna sandwich with lots of mayonnaise. Each day my mom would return home, I would act as if nothing happened, and my brother said nothing. Amazingly I was five years old and staying home. It was peaceful and fun; I had enough sense not to burn the house down.

Well, all fun had come to an end. Our nosey neighbor told my mom when she arrived home from work one day, and I overheard the conversation.

"Do you know your daughter hasn't been to school all week, and she has been staying home by herself all day?"

My mom said no, and she asked me about it. I told her Tony wouldn't show me where the bus stop was. She wasn't hearing all that, and she beat my butt good.

I went from staying at home enjoying myself to my very first interaction with a white person and a bully. Those days children stayed home alone; we were instructed not to open the door and not to lose the house key around our neck, and we did just that. We didn't have cell phones in those times, yet it felt safer.

Off to kindergarten class I go, there was already too much toxicity for a five-year-old little girl. A teacher humiliated me for talking too much in her class. She thought it was ok to put tape over my mouth for talking and made me go to another class with the tape still on my face. This went on for a while because I never stopped talking in her class. It didn't make any sense to me why teachers could talk to adults, but children could not, we had to sit there all day and listen to them babble.

I was a nervous wreck throughout school, and this boy named Frank was always picking on me in class. No authority ever tells him to stop, but I get tape on my mouth. When I would tell Frank to stop, he got upset. When he got upset, he would start fighting me when we got off the school bus. This is the first time someone from the opposite sex hit me.

The bus driver would see him beating me up and turn her head, saying nothing for months. When I found out where Frank lived, I would cry to his parents about what he did.

I will never forget that look they gave me. It's the same one Frank had, a conniving smirk. Frank did not stop his bullying.

I then decided to ask my grandmother if she would pick me up from the bus stop.

"Why? The bus stop is close to your apartment." She replied.

"This boy keeps beating me up when we get off the bus," I responded.

My grandmother asserted, "Knock the shit out of him."

My grandmother would come to pick us up from the bus stop and take us back to her place. I would look at the window at Frank with a grin thinking, "you won't beat me up today."

I was afraid to hit Frank back, I had never been in a fight and didn't know how to defend myself. After all the school fights from Frank, I had enough of riding the school bus with older children. They would tease me. One day I turned around and told this girl, "You better leave me damn lone." Other children laughed and the girl mocked, "ooh she bad."

A hurt little Black girl with no one showing her love, giving her positive guidance walking through this world with no hugs, no words of I love you, you are beautiful... she becomes lost, confused, and full of anger at times.

I could stay at home, that little Black girl was happy not going to school. Watching The Banana Split and all my other favorite shows made me happier than school. I wanted no part of school and people.

During the middle of the school year, we left Avondale Elementary school to attend B.L., this school was within walking distance from our home.

During the second part of first grade, I started opening up to playing with children in the neighborhood. I had met a few girls I liked. One friend who lived across the tracks, named Chasity, I played with her rarely. She could never leave her home and come across the tracks to play with us. Another girl named Candy lived in the same apartment complex as me. Me, Candy, and another girl would play soul train together. We would pretend we were on soul train and make up our own music and dance for hours. One day walking to school with Candy and a boy named Victor we decided to race after hearing the school bell rang. We were late anyway so we wanted to have some fun. We took off, but two steps into me running and I fell in wet mud. They laughed and kept running to school. I got up and walked back home crying.

I must have known which apartment door number to cry in front of because Candy's aunt heard me crying. She asked me what was wrong and noticed all the mud on my dress. Candy's aunt cleaned me up and gave me one of Candy's dresses to borrow.

I went on to school and of course, I was late. By the time I got to school recess was over and Music class had begun. My music teacher did not care about my reasoning for being late, she made me sit on bleacher stairs away from the other kids. When she was talking, someone was playing on their instrument, and she thought it was me so she popped my hands.

Candy and I weren't the best of friends, but one day she asked me if I want to spend the night at her house. I asked my mom and she said it was okay, so I figured no harm we do all live in the same apartments. We lived upstairs in Apartment 13; Candy lived in 3. When I arrived, Candy had other intentions than games and laughs for the night. While lying on the floor in the dark, Candy began touching my private parts inappropriately. I did not know what to do and I never told anyone. After that incident, I never played with Candy again. I made sure I steered clear of her. This was my second time, by age six, being sexually abused.

Who was supposed to be there to protect this little dark skin girl? I was small and did not know love. I received no hugs, no kisses, and was not told that I was beautiful by my parents. I was told by my grandmother and mother that I was an "ugly baby." My mom said when the nurse brought me to her, she asked whose ugly baby is this. The nurse told her it was hers. The way my mom and grandmother said that story to me, I immediately ran outside crying. They were laughing and I was crying. It was so hurtful to hear them describe me like this.

I was on the path of being damaged before I even started in life. My family described me as selfish, ugly, and hateful. This carried on for decades. It gets worse before it gets better.

I believe I loved my family more than they loved me. I protected my brothers if anyone messed with them, I was there to defend them. They never did the same for me. When Tony was in a fight with a neighborhood boy, I jumped on the boy's back to help my brother. I helped my younger brother, who is 3 years younger than me, in his first fight as well. He had started elementary school and it was my responsibility to get him off the school bus in the afternoon. One day I saw a child trying to beat him up, I told the kid to keep his hands off my little brother.

New Elementary School

I started a new one from second to fourth grade. This was a change from my first white teacher humiliating me and putting tape over my mouth, to a nice white teacher that I loved. Ms. Grace was very kind to all her students, when I graduated from high school, I went back to my elementary school in hopes to thank her. Unfortunately, she had retired and a few years later I learned she passed away. I was so heartbroken, I wanted to express my gratitude to her. I believe people need to know how they impacted your life and how much you appreciate them.

Back then, Ms. Grace suggested I repeat the second grade. I completely disagreed, but my mom agreed. Looking back this could have seemed like a conspiracy to keep children of color in the same grade, but most of my class had to repeat the grade.

Round two of second grade started, Lester Williams was in my class again. He would tease me and I would cry. I would tease him and he wanted to fight. So, one day, Ms. Grace sent us to the principal's office. The principal said the reason we were fighting was because we liked each other. Our frowns turned into blushing. After that, Lester and I began crushing on each other.

We both began to pay a lot more attention to each other. One day my grandmother picked me up from school and Lester walked me over to her car, I was so embarrassed. He said, "Bye, Daphine." Yes, "Daphine." Lester and other children had a difficult time pronouncing my name which made me dislike it. Another day, Lester rode his bike to my neighborhood and I thought it was so cute. It was nice to have a boy like me and not beat me up for a change.

Toxic Teacher

I was enjoying the second round of second grade. Turns out, I'm nearsighted and need glasses. My mother found out this was a cause to my issues with doing schoolwork. I used to sit close to the chalkboard but still misspelled a lot of words. I did not want to wear glasses; I was afraid of being teased for my appearance again. After winter break, I returned with glasses.

I preceded to take my glasses off and step on them, breaking them. I knew my cousin Charles wouldn't tell anyone about this. He laughed when he saw me breaking them.

During art class one day, my teacher Mr. Arthur and I got into it badly. I was talking in class and he pulled my ponytail. I turned around and slapped him. I didn't mean to; it was an impulse reaction. I was so angry at him for assaulting me, but I did later apologize. I liked art class; I didn't want that ruined for me too.

Summertime: This Little Girl Discovers She Loves Church

In the mid 70's and mid-'80s, I attended church a lot. My first bible was given to me by Debra, a white woman who used to take me to church with her family. Ms. Debbie had a little girl and a baby boy and her father-in-law, Mr. Griffin, was the owner of the apartment complex I lived in. I enjoyed going to Ms. Debbie's house to learn the books of the bible in order and memorizing bible verses. She always seemed to want to help me and take me under her wing. Sometimes after church, we would go out to eat or to play in Mr. Griffin's pool. Mr. Griffin was friendly to the neighborhood children, when a unit would become vacant, he would allow us to run around and play inside before it was filled again.

Ms. Debbie and her family moved away from their home, but Mr. Griffin stayed managing and operating his property for a few more years until after my family left the neighborhood. I was grateful for his kindness, and I was able to tell him goodbye and thank him.

I started to attend a different church. This church had a bus that would come pick up children on Sundays in a few different neighborhoods for bible study and fun. My brothers would sometimes join me, but they weren't into church like I was.

I went every time the bus showed up. The bus eventually stopped coming around for some reason, so I stopped attending that church.

I discovered how much I loved GOD and enjoyed attending Sunday vacation Bible School and Wednesday Bible Study. I found refuge in praising HIM. This little girl loves the LORD. I mention color a lot because most of my negative experiences at an early age came from people who looked like me.

While in the apartment stairwell, I overheard a couple talking about starting their own Wednesday bible study for children. I asked them if I could attend, and they allowed me to.

Every Wednesday night I would go sing and praise GOD and put in my offering. Pastor Whisper baptized the children who attended in the couple's tub.

After being baptized, I shared the news with my schoolmates. They laughed and I laughed with them just to fit in.

The fact that I shared my baptism with the kids got back to the pastor and his wife, who were very unhappy to hear this. The pastor's wife began rolling her eyes at me and ignoring me. I believe she was color stuck; I was the only dark skin girl in the group. She was a very bright light skin woman with what we called back then, white girl hair.

I continued to attend bible study anyway. Singing and praising GOD brought me so much joy. My favorite songs to sing were, *This Little Light of Mine* and *Going up yonder*. I could sing those songs all day. Sitting next to me in class was an older girl named Lori. I used to watch Lori belch out the words so beautifully and I would do my best to sound as good as her.

Pastor Whisper and his wife were invited to an evening event at a local church on a school night. It was a total of four girls that were invited from bible study to go along with the Whispers. I asked my mom if I could attend the event as well and she agreed.

I ran back to tell the Mrs. Whisper that my mom gave me permission to go to the event. As I was leaving, I overheard her telling her husband,

"I did not say she can come. It's not enough room for her in the car."

My feelings were hurt. I felt like I couldn't come because I was the darkest girl and the largest girl in the group. I felt even worse thinking about attending all the bible studies, offering the money I use to buy candy, and I'm not even really welcomed.

I didn't tell my mom about what Mrs. Whisper said because nothing was going to stop me from going to the event.

The night of the event, all of us girls squeezed in the back of the Whispers' car. It was tight, but we managed. Mrs. Whisper did not speak to me the entire night. Frankly, I was fine with that. Weeks later I stopped attending the bible study classes. I stopped attending church altogether for a few years after this incident.

Childhood Racism/
Stranger Danger

My grandmother Daisy moved to a beautiful new home in the early 80's. My uncle who played in the NFL purchased the home for her. The subdivision she lived in had a tennis court and a community pool. I enjoyed spending time at my grandmother's home, I used to help take care of her because she lost one of her legs to diabetes.

One weekend I stayed over at my grandmother's, and I met a girl named Lily who lived next door. We loved playing together, her brother had a cart and my brothers, and I would ride around in it.

One day she invited me into her bedroom, and I noticed she had a lot of white baby dolls. This was not surprising; I had never seen a doll that looked anything like me. Lily invited her friend Ashley over to play as well. Ashley did not acknowledge me, but I did hear her whisper to Lily,

"Tell that nigger to leave."

I didn't even know what the word nigger meant. I knew it did not sound like a nice word. Lily turned to me saying,

"I need you to leave."

I felt tears welling up in my eyes, but I was not going to let them see me cry. After that, I never knocked on her door again.

Mostly white families lived in the neighborhood with my grandmother. I quickly learned how they treated people that looked like me differently. While at the neighborhood pool, my little brother, Deon, fell while swinging on a ping-pong-like machine. He cut his ear and there was blood everywhere. I was panicking and the white adults and kids were laughing at us. No one tried to help us. I yelled at them,

"It's not funny!"

We left and walked a half-mile back to my grandmother's house.

While walking, a white man rode up next to us asking if we needed a ride home. Deon was smart with a keen intuition to sense the man was dangerous. I was ready to get in, but looking back, I'm glad Deon told him no.

I wasn't always naïve to stranger danger. A separate time, a white man drove up to a group of kids asking if we wanted to go to the Bahamas. I was the only child to walk up to the passenger side instead of the driver's side. I was spooked by his proposition. I then noticed a handgun in his passenger seat so I ran away as fast as I could. The man spun off.

I was a very trusting child when it came to adults, but they almost always were harmful towards me.

Who told little white girls they were better than little Black girls? History has divided this world by color, politics, and religion. YHWH gave us the commandments and the laws; not religions we are all HIS people.

Fun and Abuse

I enjoyed the outdoors no matter if children would play with me or not. I would get up early on a Saturday morning, brush teeth, lotion up my legs, put on a matching short set with footies with balls on the end and get to playing. My hair was always intact, full of ponytails and colorful hair bows.

Sometimes I would knock on Victor's door to go skating together. Remember him? The one that laughed when I fell during our race to school. Well, let's just say I forgave him for that and we played with each other often. When skating we both had cool and silly moves and no other kid in the neighborhood could compete with our skills. There was a skating rink two miles from my house. If Victor could not join me, I would go alone because not a lot of kids liked to go. I would stay until close sometimes.

I was an organized leader within my friend group. I planned a picnic with 15 of the neighborhood kids. I asked the girls to bring the snacks and I asked my mom to make us lemonade. I had the boys carry all the food to the park. We played, ate, and joked all day. It was an amazing day. We jumped off buildings, swings, climbed trees and played flag football.

My friends and I also enjoyed the movies. I took charge again and planned a trip to see a Bruce Lee movie and Jaws. It was such fun times, but they were short-lived because of the mental and emotional abuse.

I also took the initiative to collect soda cans and glass soda bottles. They were worth 10 cents each and could be weighed to add more money. I collected the majority of my bags and I did not want to share the money with my friends. I walked alone doing this, while they stayed in their houses. They weren't happy about this, so they kept begging until I gave them a portion of my earnings. Eventually, I stopped sharing my money, but I did share the candy I bought.

I was invited to a kid named Ben's birthday party. His family was from New York, and he had dimples and curly hair, so everyone was crushing on him. Victor's sister, Kim, came over to my house so we could go to the party together. I put on a skirt and I loved the way it looked. I was excited and happy to be invited to the party. Kim was waiting in the living room as I changed. When I left the bedroom, my mom started laughing at me. Asking me if I was really going to wear that with a nasty tone. Kim said I looked fine.

I ran back into the room crying. Kim kept asking me to come out and eventually my mother joined her. I did come out and we went to Ben's party.

I had a great time dancing. Inside, my self-esteem is caving in, especially after what just happened with my mother. However, I had so much fun that I wanted to throw a birthday party for my tenth birthday. She said I could, but it was up to me to spread the word and invite people. I told enough kids that at least three people to show up.

I had hotdogs, chips, ice cream, and cake. The whole she-bang. No one I invited even showed up. My grandmother

Daisy brought my friend Cindy, but that was it. Just my siblings, mom, grandma, and Cindy. I was really hurt, but I tried to have a great time. Cindy and I danced for hours, and we stuffed our faces with cake. This was the beginning of cake becoming a comfort food for me.

My Best Friend Sarah

A girl named Sarah moved into our neighborhood. She was a white girl, but she treated me like a sister. She never judges me and she always treated me nicely.

Sarah invited me to her birthday party, and I had a ton of fun. I invited her back a few blocks closer to my house. While hanging out, Sarah's older sister, Chica, and little brother came around the corner. I suddenly snapped and ran inside. I threw a knife, and it struck the baby's head. Chica ran screaming and her little brother was screaming, and everyone was looking in disbelief. My mother wasn't home, but I was scared. I was grateful no adults were around to have me taken away. When my mom got home and learned about this, she did beat me until I ran under my bed screaming.

Fortunately, Sarah's parents did not press charges and they allowed us to stay friends. However, they wouldn't allow Sarah to come outside all the time like they used to. But I could come into her bedroom and play for just 15 minutes. Sarah and her family moved away by the time I started third grade.

After months of being gone Sarah's mother came back to the neighborhood to visit with an old friend. I was feeling sad, wishing Sarah was with her mom. Turns out, she was! I looked up and like a miracle from GOD, Sarah was walking towards our apartment. We both ran towards each other and shared a big hug with tears. I miss Sarah to this day. My older brother would tease that I liked Sarah more than my own family. However, Sarah never treated me nasty like my family often did.

Divided Siblings

My siblings and I were never as close as I would have liked. I noticed the differences in treatment from our mother. She would say she wished she had three boys. I was always told I needed to lose weight or that I'm fat. My older brother would call me ugly. Deon was the baby and he was light skin along with Tony, so they received the best love from my mother. Sometimes when sitting on the couch together, Tony would say,

"I don't want this ugly girl sitting next to me. Don't touch me, ugly girl."

It would hurt me deeply, but I played like I was laughing it off. Tony would always remind me that he thought I was fat and ugly.

Our dad was stationed in the Army when he sent me a beautiful yellow silk blanket. I was extremely excited to receive something from my dad. Soon enough, my mom allowed my brothers to use it and to sleep on it. I tried taking it away, but my mom let them keep it and they destroyed the blanket. My dad also bought me a 10-speed bike for my birthday. Deon wanted to ride the bike without even asking and I told him no, you can't ride it. My mother struck me so hard in the head I felt like I was dying. All I could do was cry. My Aunt Diana was visiting at the time and she asked my mother why she hit me like that just because I don't want Deon riding my bike. My mother responded saying I was selfish and hateful. But I was actually always helpful and always cherished the things that were given to me. I usually had no problem sharing if my things were treated with respect.

Generational Hurt

My mom shared a story of how her mom used to always praise her little brother as he was the only son. He would get anything and everything he wanted, and her sisters would have much of nothing.

My grandmother Daisy shared the story of how her dad did not like her and just wanted to marry her off, which was difficult.

> *Do People want to change? When you know better, you do better. When you do not do better, it's time for a self-check-in.*
> *"Sometimes you do not know why you do the things you do until you are analyzing your past intentionally strip of our identity." Song of Solomon 1:5-6*

School Bully and Black Hateful Teachers

Summer ended and I am excited about starting the third grade. I wasn't thrilled about still wearing glasses, but it did help me in class. While sitting at my desk, I looked up and there's Lester from second grade. I did not want him in the same class as me because I was self-conscious with my glasses.

"Hi Daphine." Lester said as he sat down.

I blushed back at him. Melissa from second grade was also in our class. She was a good friend to play with and have in class.

Then a girl comes in and sits behind my desk. By the way she was looking at me, I could tell she was going to make this a difficult year. She hit the back of my chair saying, "Don't push that chair on my foot."

I looked at her in disgust with no words. I figured this would be my new bully, but there would be no daily fights this time around.

When class begins, we go around introducing ourselves. Turns out the little menace behind me is Tisha.

As the days go by, Tisha spreads rumors about me all around our class. Luckily, Lester ignored this nonsense. He would write me notes asking if I liked him, Yes or No. Of course, I would circle yes.

One day Tisha got ahold of one of the notes and started making fun of Lester for liking me.

During recess, she would have a group of girls that she controlled go around bullying people. I would have liked to be her friend, but I was not going to follow someone's commands like that blindly.

Tisha would bully Melissa too. Melissa would ask me to protect her, and I would. Another student used me like a bodyguard, an Asian boy named John. He was funny and friendly to me, so I did not mind. He did not speak great English, but I always understood him, and we remained great friends.

Tisha was the least of my problems, our teacher Ms. Cobb was very unfriendly to me and I didn't understand why.

We had a classroom for mentally disabled students who sometimes wore helmets and would be seemingly nasty to other children. Back then, we called them retarded. During lunch, they would walk up to your table and snatch your food off of your tray. Or stick their fingers all in your food. They usually did this to kids at the ends of the table. They never messed with kids that brought their own food.

Ms. Cobb knew I did not want to sit at the end of the lunch table, but she would put me there almost daily.

I had a difficult time with math. Math time was for 45 minutes every day. Ms. Cobb would choose different students to work out a math problem on the board. When she chose me, it would take me a while to solve the problem and Ms. Cobb would become irrationally angry. She would grab my head and start hitting me and wiggling my head around. I would cry and be so embarrassed. I didn't even want to look at the children, afraid they wouldn't feel sorry for me and just laugh. After the embarrassment, Ms. Cobb would allow the kids to help me with the problem.

The third grade could not have ended fast enough. I was glad to get away from Ms. Cobb and Tisha. Hold up, turns out I haven't left these toxic people behind. In fourth grade I was in class with Tisha again. My new teacher was Ms. Dennis who was also awful. Melissa, John, and Lester were also in the class so that was nice seeing them. Lester was still writing me love notes, so I guess we were still dating.

Tisha would bully Melissa by taking her chips from her lunch box. This happened almost daily and Melissa would give them up each time.

Ms. Dennis was no better than Ms. Cobb. Ms. Dennis would physically and emotionally abuse me publicly as well. They made me fear the subject of math. Ms. Dennis did the same horrible abuse to me when I was trying to work out a math problem. I just cried from the pain and embarrassment. After lunch I would have to try the problem again. Unlike Ms. Cobb, she made me do it by myself while she yelled.

There was a new fourth grade teacher hired at our school. I wished and wished that I would be selected to move to her class. I was tired of all this abuse from these adults who decided I was not worthy of compassion and love. One of the students that got to leave was Lester. It was bittersweet, at least he wouldn't see me get hurt like that anymore.

During lunch, Ms. Dennis would look at me with disgust in her eyes. The mentally disabled children started licking their fingers and then touching your food saying,

"You want that?" While laughing.

I truly believed they had some sense not to do that but knew they wouldn't get in much trouble.

During all of this abuse, there was some light. Melissa and I received a Spanish-speaking award. I was great at Spanish class, and I caught on very well. I also enjoyed going to music class where I was encouraged to sing and learn the clarinet. I even performed at our school's Christmas concert. My mother came and watched me perform. It made me feel proud and important. This was my last year at this school because we were moving, I'm glad I got some good memories out of it.

114 North West 4th Street

My mother met a man a lot older than her named Winston. Sometimes we would all spend the night in his apartment. Winston kept a clean home and vehicle. This was the first we had ever been in an apartment with an air conditioner. Winston seemed like a nice man. My brothers and I got to sleep on a soft bed. I would always wet the bed and when I would wake Winston up with this information and he would whip me with a belt every time. I would stop waking him in fear and eventually I stopped wetting the bed.

My mother gave up her apartment and we moved in with Winston in a two-bedroom apartment. It was in a nice neighborhood. Winston was a great cook. Once a week he would prepare T-bone steaks with baked potatoes.

After school, Winston would have a sandwich waiting for me and my siblings, four cookies, and some milk as a snack before dinner.

Every two weeks Winston would take my brothers to the barbershop and me to Ms. Flossie's house. She was the woman that would press my grandmother's hair. Ms. Flossie would do my hair and she got my hair growing even longer. With Winston, we had more clothes to wear and money didn't seem like an issue.

Winston was a strict disciplinarian stepfather though. Three times you come inside from playing and he would not let you back out. I didn't pay attention to this rule so one day after the third time of coming in he made me stay inside. I cried in my room but eventually, I jumped out the window to continue playing.

Winston decided to take us to the county fair, but before we went, we had to stop at my grandmother's house. I wanted to go inside with my mom to see my grandmother. Winston said I could not go and if I left the car, he was going to leave me. I was thinking, yeah right, he is not my daddy. So went inside with my mom and when we returned, he told me I could not get back in the car. I had to stay, and they drove off as I cried.

My brothers never got a whooping from Winston, but I got a few beatings when I peed the bed. I also got beat for something that I cannot recall, but I do remember the belt striking me terribly hard.

Ultimately, Winston and I became a duo. He took us on a family trip to Disney World and Bush Garden. We had such great fun and got to eat at several nice restaurants.

But Winston brought me back to what my dad said to me. He would tell me to stop singing. He said, "I need to know this schoolwork like I know these songs." He did not understand that singing fed my soul. He didn't know I was doing my best and all the trauma I had to endure while doing my best.

Another New Neighborhood
with Winston

We lived in with Winston for four years before we moved again to a larger place. I kept telling Winston I wanted my own bedroom and he made it happen. In our new neighborhood, we also had a big backyard and our own washer and dryer. My room had a dresser, mirror, and a queen-size bed. My mom and I hung all of my school awards on the wall.

The neighborhood was nice and most of the families were white families. No children would really come outside. Later I met some girls around my age, but they were heavy into the video game system Atari. We had cable, so not a lot of video games because a video games system was not allowed.

Playing with these kids was totally different. I had my first fight with a high school girl that was twice my size. She had two sisters. My brother liked one of the sisters and she told me to tell him, "We don't do Black boys."

During the fight, the older girl got in a lot more hits than me. After the fight, I told her my cousins goes to her school and I was going to tell them to beat her up. She had nothing but fear on her face. The next day she tried being much nicer to me.

We didn't fit in the neighborhood very well. We enjoyed R&B music and rap; this was the first-time hearing rock n' roll music. It wasn't a very fun neighborhood; we spent more time with our grandmother because of this.

It was time for me to start school at my final elementary school in fifth grade. It was called Campbell Drive. My mom received a letter in the mail detailing where my class would be held and who my teacher was. Ms. Turner was her name. I did not know what to expect, but I was praying for the best.

Upon arriving to school, I got to know a few white and Hispanic girls. They were into smoking cigarettes and dating boys. I did not fit in at all. Tina and the other girls looked way older than a fifth-grader. Her body was much more developed than mine. One of the girls, Dawn, lived in a trailer park near us and sometimes we would walk home together. While walking home one day Dawn was smoking a cigarette and she asked if I wanted to try it. I took a puff and quickly realized it was not for me.

Another day, Dawn came over to my house. She complimented our house for being clean and nice, but she determined that,

"All Black people have glass in their house."

I didn't really know what she meant by that, and I didn't say anything back about it. She was a popular white girl, and I didn't want to jeopardize our budding friendship.

To fit in with the other girls I would defend Dawn when someone was messing with her. A girl from another class was talking mess to us and I told her to stop, she put her finger in front of my face and I slapped her. My principal Mr. Oliver found out and said I could either get three licks with the wood paddle or ten days suspension. I chose the paddle because I knew I would get much worse from my mother and stepfather if I gotten days of suspension.

This new school opened my personality. The fifth graders were able to volunteer to read to the kindergarteners and help teachers grade their papers. I really enjoyed it and decided I wanted to be a teacher.

I went almost the entire school year with Ms. Turner and no problems. She hardly got out of her seat, she just sat chewing gum with her arms folded. She didn't say much to me. I could tell she liked the other girls more than me. Maybe it was my appearance that wasn't to her liking. I had gained a lot of weight from third to fifth grade and I began to compare my looks to the other girls.

I put myself on a diet of white bread and cookies and quickly found out that was not working. When left alone at home I would open my bible and begin singing the verses. I would cry feeling the spirit. I would sometimes look up and yell at GOD, waving my middle finger, asking,

"Why would you make me so dark, fat and ugly!"

I was so angry. Family and Black teachers did not make me feel beautiful or worthy of love from anyone. Before fifth grade ended, I did not get out of there unscathed. I didn't do anything, and Ms. Turner got up from her chair and hit me on the top of the head with a lot of force. I sat there and cried as the children stared. I never felt safe or protected as a child by an adult or person.

The other children came to my defense saying that I wasn't the one talking during the lesson. She did not care, nor did she apologize. I was humiliated and felt like crap. Words truly cannot describe how much it still hurts to know these Black teachers were more than okay with abusing a little Black girl.

I Am Not Your Punching Bag

At this point, who am I? So much has happened by the age of 12. My older cousin Jane made me her punching bag because she simply did not like me.

The first incident was at my grandmother's house. I touched something of Jane's, and she punched me. The second time, we were at a wrestling tournament with our other cousin Charles. I sat in the bleachers, doing nothing. Jane offered me a sip of her drink and I took it. She said I drank too much, and she punched me extremely hard in the back. I arched my back and could barely catch my breath. She threatened me again to not scream with all the people around. Even Charles asked why she punched me like that.

If I even moved wrong, Jane would be ready to put her hands on me. I told my mom about all of this, and my mother never addressed Jane about this.

Winston and my mother wanted some time alone for the summer, so they drove us to Fort Pierce, Florida to the house of Aunt Josie and her daughter Jane. The first Saturday of being there, Aunt Josie took us to the church where she was a Seven Day Adventist. I preferred watching cartoons on Saturday morning, but we had to go. The church was putting a program together for the children to be a part of and my aunt volunteered me to join. I did not know any of these kids, so I was not that thrilled about it. My aunt didn't even volunteer my brothers, just me.

I did not know the words to the songs, so I just lip-synced through the whole program. I was embarrassed.

My stepfather and mom gave my aunt money to feed us for two weeks. We ate good the first few days. My aunt even let me help her make homemade strawberry ice cream. She also threw a birthday party for Deon on July 23. All the neighborhood children attended.

While on the porch, I took a ball from my brother, and he wanted me to give it back, but I said I had it first. My aunt proceeded to get a belt and beat me at the birthday party. I was jumping and screaming. She made me go inside and I could not attend the party any longer.

During our last week at my aunt's house, I was about ready to get out of there. Jane was teasing me about my looks, and I called her a prostitute. Jane hit me like she always does, and her mother said and did nothing. However, when my parents picked us up Aunt Josie made sure to tell them what I called Jane. Fortunately, my parents were still in a happy mood, so they did not discipline me. The next summer Aunt Josie did not want me coming to her house because I was, "too bad." I told my stepfather I do not care; I didn't want to go anyway.

He replied sternly, "Never use those words, 'I don't care.'" But I truly did not care.

Back to Church Where There's My Serenity

The summer before moving on to the sixth grade, we received flyers in our neighborhood about a summer vocational bible school at New Baptist Church. It was Monday thru Friday for six weeks free, just be outside in front of your home by 7:30am and the bus would pick you up. They didn't require a parent's signature to sign up, so I just attended. I never missed a day for six weeks. The first week there were about five of us who attended. By the second week, I was basically the only child. Sometimes this little white girl would show up, but I was the only Black person and the only consistent child there. I did not mind at all, I had so much fun singing the songs, doing arts and crafts, and they gave us lunch each day. I didn't want it to end. For me, this was a place of peace, a safe place.

Molested By Another Cousin

During the summer before sixth grade, my family went to Georgia. This is where my family history started, as far as we know. We went for a family reunion, months after I'd turned 13. I had a lot of fun with my younger cousins and the ones my age. My favorite cousin was Onica. She asked me to spend the night with her and I did. We slept in the same twin bed in her bedroom. Late in the night, I heard someone come into the room, I laid there quiet and still. I peeped to see who it was, and I saw his face. It was my grandmother's sister's son. I pretended to sleep as he took my hand and put it on his private parts. I was terrified. The only thing I could think to do was move so he thought I was waking up and he ran away. I never told my mom, but I did tell Jane many years later. She thought I should just forgive and forget. The story basically went on deaf ears.

I Am Appreciative

As a child and now as an adult, I never expected anyone to give me anything or do anything for me. I always wanted to earn it. I loved cleaning our home, my grandmother's home, and the homes of the friends I frequently visited.

To earn money from my stepfather to buy cookies at school or have money to go to the skating rink, I would offer to do an extra chore around the house. I would vacuum the entire house, wash the dishes, clean the tub, or make my parent's bed.

One boring Saturday I asked Winston if I made his bed every day for a week if I could get $3.50 to go to the skating rink today. He gladly accepted and I walked two miles on a hot Florida day to the rink and skated all day. When it was time to go, I passed out in the grass, probably from a lack of water. I only ate breakfast that day. I don't know how long I was there, but eventually; I woke up and just continued home.

You Got to be Kidding Me

I started middle school and none other than Tisha is at the same school. My homeroom and math class I shared with her. How in the hell did this girl get back in my life? She picked up immediately where she had left off with her smug looks. The next surprise is Lester. He walks in and my mouth dropped. I am with my elementary school crush and bully all over again. They watched me get abused in math class and here we are again, in now, Ms. Oliver's math class.

I did my best to not communicate with Tisha or Lester on the first day of school. I was already nervous about the sixth grade. Tisha and Lester seemed to know a lot of the kids in our homeroom class.

I found some new friends in class. Doris was one of them. She was laid back, kind of lazy, but very supportive. We also talked with some random white and Hispanic girls at times. Tisha tried to act like she had changed and wanted to be friends, but it was just a trick. She had other girls saying my lips were too dark, they called me four eyes, and they talked about my hairstyles and clothing choices.

My hair always seemed to be on Tisha's mind. Even back in elementary school. Tisha's mom used to work at the cafeteria in elementary school and she would always compliment my hair, asking me who did it. I got my press every two weeks. It was Black, long, and it was beautiful. Tisha and her squad would tease me about my hairstyles, but they would try to copy them the next day.

Tisha didn't really look like a sixth grader, and she didn't try to. The kids would call her bumpy face and big booty, big tits. She embraced the big booty name, but not so much the bumpy face name.

Lester became a bully as well. He said my knees were large and Tisha joined in on the teasing. She also went in on my hair. I told her, "You can say what you want about my hair, but you better not put your hands on me."

She was furious. The kids were laughing and fueling us to fight, and she wanted to.

During gym class, we broke off into teams to play softball. Tisha didn't like the way I was pitching the ball, so she stomped her way over to me, swishing her hips. I didn't really hear anything she was saying, but she started waving her finger in my face. By this point, you know I hate having fingers shoved into my face. I slapped her finger down and told her to keep it out of my face. She acted like she wanted to hit me, and I told her I wasn't scared, I stood there watching. P.E. came to an and we both proceeded to the locker room.

Romans 1:26-27
Children will absorb the negative before the positive. We as parents rarely introduce our children to our Creator before fast foods, cartoons, etc. Most of us are guilty of this.

On the way to the locker room, I was dumbfounded. I saw Candy. She was the little girl that had molested me. She was now in eighth grade, and it was her class's turn to go to the gym. We locked eyes, but we didn't acknowledge one another. That was the last time I took a shower in the locker room. My reading teacher, Ms. Garcia, took notice saying, "All must have had gym class today." Basically, saying I stank.

I took notice of the girls with Candy, including the women's basketball coach whom all looked and acted like hard boys. The term we used back then was, "bull dykes."

Another time I saw this behavior is with two ladies in my neighborhood. My friend Kizzy, who was much younger than me, had two moms. Kizzy's mother was white, and her mother's mate was a Black woman named Betty. When I was playing with her in the yard, I saw the two women kissing. I told her that her mom was kissing Betty. She replied,

"That's my daddy!"

I immediately responded,

"Girl, that is not your daddy, that's a woman!"

Her mother saw and heard what Kizzy had said and she ran over to us to downplay what she had said.

Sixth Grade Comes to an End

It was just a few months before school would end and Doris and I became better friends. The only thing about Doris is, she likes to skip class. Her parents didn't force her to attend. Her excuse would be an asthma attack. That didn't make sense though, when I saw her on the days she did not attend, she was always outside playing.

Ms. Levington taught us language arts in the second period and science in the fourth period. When Tisha and her squad were walking out laughing about hairstyle, Ms. Levington looked as though she noticed, and she was going to intervene. However, the bell rang, and it was all forgotten. Doris decided she was not going to third or fourth period and she invited me to skip with her. I said sure. I didn't think it was a big deal at first, but then I got caught skipping while in the bathroom. Doris left me and she didn't get caught. So much for friendship. I was taken to Ms. Levington's class who gave me a very disapproving look.

I got three days in-school suspension for skipping. I told my mom what had happened and to not be mad, but she looked like she had bigger problems to deal with.

Tisha's final attempt to hurt me was creating a slam book. Slam books are negative comments about someone's character or appearance. Fortunately, it didn't spread as much she thought it would.

I ended sixth grade on a high note and I was extremely grateful that Tisha was going back to Mississippi for good.

Shoe Man Jack and His Daughter

Shoe man Jack and his daughter entered our lives briefly by the end of my sixth-grade year. A business acquaintance of my mother's introduced her to the man. Jack needed someone to help him return shoes to his customers. He worked 40 minutes away from the area most of the customers resided in and my mother helped him return those shoes. Jack introduced me to his daughter, Elia, and we went skating together.

Friends come and go, especially when you're young. I wanted acceptance so I was almost always open to meeting new kids.

My mother warned me to be on my best behavior and to be kind to Elia. When I returned, I told my mom how Elia was not on her best behavior and was not very nice to me.

Cancer & Another Life Change

Our household started changing when my stepfather's attitude towards us changed. He didn't seem to want us around anymore. Tony would be running late for school and Winston would simply leave him in the house. I don't think Tony wanted to be driven to school anymore since he was getting older, but I still didn't like Winston just leaving him behind like that. My stepfather and mother did not argue, but one day I did hear the tension in their voice during a conversation.

I was not happy when Winston departed from our lives, I never thought he would abandon us. My love for him was pure and abundant. I did not understand the pain I was feeling. We moved into a one-bedroom apartment. One of my last conversations with him was when he visited us looking to borrow the vacuum.

"Bring me the vacuum, Delphina."

In a curt tone, I responded, "come get it yourself." I was so angry with Winston, he meant so much to me.

Before leaving, Winston asked my mother to come back. She declined because of how the relationship ended. I wish she had taken him back.

I never saw Winston again. The last time my mother had seen him was when she received a call from his friend explaining that Winston was in the hospital. He was dying of cancer. This was my first time hearing the word cancer.

A Stepfather's and Stepdaughter's Love

I adored my stepfather. We used to dance together and have pillow fights. We would do simple tasks like grocery shopping or cleaning, and it was always so fun. He even used to defend me from my mom's rude remarks. We laughed together and would rub each other's stinky feet. When I asked him a question, he didn't want to answer, he would laugh and say, "putting tang."

He was a great stepfather, person, and disciplinarian. I enjoyed the time we spent together and sadly it all came to an end much too soon.

My favorite words from my stepfather were to never say, "I don't care." These words have stuck by me.

Fatal Call

That fatal call came in August of 1984. I answered the phone and a nurse on the other end said,

"I am sorry, but Winston has passed away."

She didn't even ask for an adult before laying this horrible news on the receiver. I did not know how to take it. My stepfather is gone. I walked back outside and sat next to my friend Victor on the steps. I never even told Winston I loved him. I showed it to him, but never said those words. I know he's with me in spirit and not a year goes by, I do not dream of him.

Back to the Old Neighborhood and a New Middle School

This move was like the Jefferson TV show except instead of moving up we were moving down. We went from a three-bedroom nice home to a one-bedroom apartment. My mother was waiting on a two-bedroom to become available. The new school for Tony and me was within walking distance. Many of the children that attended, we knew from our grandmother's neighborhood. It had been so long that I felt out of place.

I had gained more weight again. My mother gave each of us $100 to go school shopping. It wasn't enough for me because I wanted the name brands jeans that a lot of girls were wearing. Buying those jeans ate up most of my money so I could only afford a few shorts and three other pairs of pants and one pair of shoes for the whole school year. It was difficult for my mother to fully provide for us.

My dad did not help my mother financially or emotionally. It wasn't like he was unable to provide, he simply only cared about himself. My father benefitted from the Army and by using his kids' names to secretly get more financial assistance.

The first week of school, I quickly ran out of clothes. I wore the Dache jeans twice that week, hoping no one would notice.

I also learned that the Black girls didn't even wear Dache jeans at this school. They wore matching colorful outfits of which, I had none. I was trying to fit in as much as possible.

I asked my mom for my first relaxer, only because all the other girls had one, and I returned to school with a ton of confidence. That is, until we had gym class outside during the next nine weeks of school in the hot Florida sun, which all but ruined my relaxed hair. I chose to do modern dance so I could be inside with the AC.

I chose to continue to pursue modern dance, it was something I was good at, and I enjoyed it. I began to lose weight because of the exercise. Some girls would act jealous or rude towards me. Victor began to take more notice of me. Somehow, we just fell into a relationship with each other.

Victor became my protector due to other girls wanting to fight me and cause problems. Tony didn't like Victor liking me and would say, "why are you dating my ugly sister?"

Seventh grade was a terrible school year, I was teased and mocked. Many girls were just mean to me. Through it all, I kept my head held high. I was happy when the school year ended. I got out with just two fights and a few fake friendships.

Shoe Man Jack Returns

Shoe man Jack had returned after my stepfather passed away. I didn't think anything of it until he started calling my house. Often. Asking for my mom, at that. He never introduced himself with a label and my mom never called him her boyfriend. We just saw him around more and more.

My grandmother didn't like him and neither did I. Months into their relationship, Jack's calls became more and more irritating. These calls would typically go like this,

"Hello?"

"Hi, where's your mom?"

"I don't know."

Eventually, I would end the call with,

"If she wanted you to know where she was, she would have told you." Click.

He started complaining to my mom that I was rude to him. Well, I didn't like him and I was making that clear. My mom was struggling, and Jack wasn't any help so his attention in our lives just didn't feel right to me.

Jack started sleeping over in our small two-bedroom apartment. He stayed in the room I shared with my mom. I was 14 and this grown man was basically sharing a room with me. He had his own place so I never understood this.

After a while, my mom's attention was solely on working and Jack. Her attitude towards me became much worse as one day she exclaimed,

"You not going to stop me from being happy. You must be jealous that Jack is buying me clothes and getting my hair done."

Stunned, all I could respond with was, "Why can't you just be my mom? I just want to talk to you." Of course, this sentiment went on deaf ears.

Jack, along with his daughter, made my life even more toxic. My mother clearly preferred his daughter over me and would often put her on a pedestal above me. Jack did nothing for me and my siblings.

Victor's Sister Visits

I asked my mom if Victor's sister, Kathy, could sleep over. Fortunately, she allowed it. The night began quite well. Kathy and I were seated at the dinner table, in front of the meal my mom had prepared for us. The night turned dark fast.

My mom said something regarding Jack, and I mumbled a smart comment under my breath. My mom proceeded to get up from the table, walk over to me, and begin beating me over the head right in front of Kathy.

I was in hysterics. I suggested that Kathy leave, and she agreed. We walked back to her house silently.

Eighth Grade Rising

The summer before eighth grade was one of the best summers. Victor, Tony, and I all got jobs at Burger World working 40 hours a week. We were getting paid and loving it. We bought new clothes, any food we liked, we visited the mall and went skating all the time.

I also joined a dance program in which I was able to create some of the choreography we performed. Performing felt so good, especially when my mom would be in the audience. The crowd would go wild when me and the other girls would hit the dance floor smoothly and quickly. Today, I would have loved to show my granddaughters their young grandma dancing like nobody's watching.

By this time, Victor and I grew even closer. I loved him deeply and he loved me. He treated me like I was special, no one else ever really did this. We would be on the phone for hours, sometimes just listening to each other breathe.

Victor did have his cons now. When it came to my elementary school crush Lester, Victor could be quite jealous and slightly abusive. I hadn't even seen Lester since sixth grade, but when we did lock eyes again, at the skating rink it was clear he had feelings for the new me. Victor noticed this connection and he took my hand and bent my pinky bad that I teared up.

Despite having an overall positive relationship, participating in activities in school, and working, I still felt empty. Low self-esteem has a way of always being in the background when your soul isn't being nurtured. Doris and Melissa from sixth grade attended the same junior high. I liked being their friends, but we were never as close as I would have liked.

I did meet two other girls, Toya and Wanda. Me, Doris, Toya, and Wanda became the four musketeers. Even though I had lost weight, I could not help but compare myself to these girls. They were thinner and lighter than me, and to me, at the time, that meant they were more beautiful than me. I never heard those words, "you're pretty…I love you…" Those were foreign to me. Of course, Victor would say those things but it's not the same as your parents or family indulging you.

I was always seeking out acceptance. My eighth-grade teacher, Ms. Evans, was another older Black woman. I did not know what to expect, considering the other teachers I had were incredibly toxic. Fortunately, Ms. Evans was different. I was called her classroom pet because I didn't mind helping her in any way I could. I made sure to complete all the work she assigned on time, I volunteered to answer questions in class, and I even would stay back and help her clean up her classroom. One day she said,

"Your mother must be proud of you because you're so helpful and kind."

I honestly had to hold back tears. I simply said, "yes ma'am." No woman that looked like me had said anything so nice to me.

In these low confidence times, I was leaning heavily on Victor. By this time, I'm 16. And I'm pregnant. Although I was scared,

I was happy too. I would have a baby I could adore and love and who would adore and love me back. I knew this baby would not judge me like the rest of the world did.

In Spring, my 7th grade school year I was riding a bike my dad had brought me. Victor was watching me and all of a sudden, he was yelling my name. Then BANG! I was struck by a vehicle driven by an old white man. He stayed on the scene and others nearby helped me. I was unconscious for a long while until they brought me to the hospital. My mom and my cousin Jane came to the hospital, my dad later joined. However, Victor stayed by my side in a helpful and loving way. The doctor said the massive bruise on my leg needed to be massaged and the bandage changed often. Victor did just that.

I felt like Victor was my savior sometimes. I would tell him we should run away to New York and live somewhere that we can feel free and on top of the world. Of course, this never came to fruition.

My Hair Is Like My Life

My hair was on the minds of many adults and children. As a little girl, my mother did not know how to style my hair. I went through stages just like in my life. After the sores and dandruff, to hot comb presses, to long thick ponytails filled with colorful hair bows.

The girls at school envied my hair and envied my smooth skin tone. I wanted to fit in with the other girls, so I asked my mom to relax my hair, just like theirs. My hair changed again, I now knew what a jheri curl was, many of the girls were getting them. My dad took me to his girlfriend's house for the chemical installation. I stayed there for hours only to have my hair break off, then I needed it all to be cut off. My hair grew back thick and beautiful once again. Still, like my life, I am not happy with my hair. Weekly hair salon trips to cut my hair and every day long for a better life. My Hair is Like My Life.

No More Childhood

In 1985, I started the ninth grade. I'm excited about this fresh start with new kids and a new environment. I stopped working at Burger World fortunately. They had me, Tony, and Victor working adult hours. The company eventually faced legal punishment for breaking child labor laws.

On the first day of school, I needed to ride the school bus. I hadn't ridden the school bus since fourth grade. I was nervous and self-conscious; kids would stare at me, and they wouldn't move over so I could sit down. After a few months of catching the bus, I decided to switch to public transportation in the morning and the school bus in the afternoon. Eventually, a girl did start making fun of my eyes on the afternoon ride.

Victor was on the wrestling team and would practice for long hours after school. We would see each other during pass time, and he would sometimes walk me to class. Melissa and Juan attended the same high school, we would occasionally speak, but nothing beyond that. I would have liked to have lunch with them.

There were a lot of kids from my grandmother's neighborhood in the high school. They were in the tenth and eleventh grades and they were close. I would have been in the tenth grade, and Tony and Victor in the eleventh had we not been held back all those years ago.

After Christmas break, I noticed I was gaining more weight. I didn't think anything of it because I always losing and gaining. It hurt me when Victor relayed the message that his mom thought I was getting fat.

On Valentine's Day, the school was selling note grams that would be delivered to the recipient's classroom. To my surprise, Victor bought me one and it did make me happy.

Branching out from being under Victor so much, I was able to meet a new acquaintance. Her name was Yolanda. She was much more mature as she had her own car and a boyfriend. We hit it off very well.

Everything changed in the spring. I try out for the track team and enjoy myself very much. Doris and I even had a chance at modeling with an agency. Then, the other shoe dropped. I'm pregnant. Victor told his mom, and she was not happy, of course.

I continued to attend my high school for a few weeks and eventually, I enroll in a school for expecting teenaged mothers. My math teacher there, Ms. Harper, was very kind and concerned.

In middle school, they taught us about women's bodies, but not much about pregnancy. It was never discussed. My mother asked me one day,

"Why didn't you tell me you were having sex? And when I asked if you were, why did you say no?"

I didn't have a response for her. You're reading this book, there was no strong mother and daughter relationship between us.

As time passes, Victor and I see each other, but not as much. My mom doesn't hold back on declaring he is going to make a fool out of me.

The school was going okay. I received a D in typing class. I didn't understand why. I went to the principal, telling them I've been typing since the third grade, how dare this lady give me a D. I was with child and still wanted to be a child.

Going to school while pregnant was unreal. One day I actually went blind while waiting for the bus to go to school. I called my mom in a panic and she advised that I stay home from school that day.

Victor and I weren't spending much time together. Sometimes he would take me to get baby items, but that's about it. One day, his car broke down. That was one of the greatest laughs, watching him get frustrated trying to figure out how to fix it. It would be a long time before I laughed like that again. I was alone for most of my pregnancy. My mom attended the first doctor's appointment and that was her last. Victor came to none.

On August 9th, 1986, I had a checkup scheduled. The baby was due on the 4th and it hadn't arrived yet. I walked myself to the clinic. It was a hot day in the summer in Florida. Victor had a new nice, light blue car, and he drove right past me. Almost like he didn't even know me.

On August 10th, I went into labor. I did not have insurance so I could not afford the $500 to stay in the hospital and wait for the baby to come. Victor took me back home, but eventually, I had to return to the hospital. This time, Victor's stepfather and his mother, drove me and my mother to the hospital where I had a beautiful baby boy. Victor didn't even come.

A Gift is Born

My son, KJ, is born. Fortunately, my mom was in the hospital with me, she made me feel like everything is going to be okay. I prayed my son would be healthy and happy. He came out light skin with nice hair, which I also prayed for. I did not want him to be dark like me. I was described as ugly by so many people; I did not want that for KJ. He had to stay in the hospital for an additional two weeks until he could hold down the baby formula.

Shoe Man Jack picked us up from the hospital. Victor had a car but had no interest. I looked homeless and felt homeless. I was wearing an old dress, no panties, no bra…I couldn't even take my baby home until he was healthy enough.

When I arrived home, the stitches gave me unbearable pain. I started walking more to lose weight and distract myself from the pain. The pregnancy really tortured my body, and I couldn't even hold my baby. I called the hospital every day to check on him. On the thirteenth day, I asked Jack to take me to the hospital to see him. I whispered in KJ's ear to please stop throwing up. Jack saw us together and asked if I was sure they gave me the right baby. He was mean and it was uncalled for. The next day, however, I received a call that KJ could come home.

I was thrilled my baby boy could come home to me; I missed him dearly. What I was not in for, was the incredible amount of stress that would ensue.

Victor's family came over to see the family and they were excited. A childhood friend of mine offered to throw a baby shower for me. I told her no, I was afraid no one would come, just like my tenth birthday party. I could not handle the disappointment if no one showed up.

I needed money to provide for KJ and Victor gave me $30 a week for 4 weeks. It stopped when he got involved with a pregnant girl from Georgia. Victor spent all his free time with her. It didn't make sense to me. I had seen the girl, Jezebel, at school.

Jezebel was assigned to read and sing nursery rhymes to the babies one day. The same day Victor was visiting her (and not his child).

I was not going to let this happen, I made it clear I didn't want her touching my baby.

The principal brought both me and Jezebel to the office over this matter.

Principal Clark started,

"What is going on between you two girls?"

I explained, "My son's dad is here to see her and we have a baby together. I do not want those two-playing house with my baby."

Principal Clark turned to Jezebel,

"Why are you talking to her son's father?"

Jezebel was hardly concerned with her answer,

"We are just friends; he wants to take me to the movies."

Principal Clark kind of snapped at that,

"You don't think he will do what he's done to Delphina, to you? What makes you think you are any better or any different?"

All this went on deaf ears as Jezebel simply thought Victor was just being friendly.

Victor stopped providing and I decided to go to court and put him on child support. I would watch him, out my window, walking to Jezebel's house with no regard to me. I cried and cried, wondering how someone I grew up with, could be so harsh to me and his son.

The government would garnish Victor's wages to pay me child support but the money was so little, it hardly helped. My mom learned to drive so she could transport KJ back and forth from the small number of babysitters I had lined up. My cousin Shelly would babysit him for a few months before she moves to Georgia. My aunt Issa helped as well.

The energy and tension in my mom's house were overly negative. She even suggested I give my baby up for adoption to my aunt. I told her no way am I giving my baby up to anyone.

I felt my son and I was becoming a burden, her attitude toward me got hostile to the point she would no longer wash my son and my clothes. I had no money for the coin laundromat, so here I am crying hand washing our clothes in the bathtub, my mother started allowing Jack to stay over more in our small two-bedroom apartment. Things were tense, I mentioned to my mom don't leave rat poison behind the couch. She looked at me and told me,

"This my damn house, you don't tell me what not to leave."

I was hurt by her words; I knew me and KJ needed to get out of her house. Before Tony moved to Georgia, at 1am, my mother threw me and my son out on the porch. I was sobbing, we stayed outside for a few hours before she finally allowed us back inside. How did I bring a child into the world and I'm already not feeling good about myself or the places I'm staying in.

Jack's daughter had moved into our place as well. I asked my mom why; she has a mother. My mom started comparing me and Elia again. She talked of her as pretty, doing well for herself, among other things. I believe she did those things to hurt me. Anytime Jack or Elia was around, my mom's attitude changed nasty towards me.

One day, my nine-month-old son was crawling and Elia stepped on him, causing him to cry out. I started yelling at her, then she pushed me and I attacked her head and we began fighting. I wanted to kill the girl. After that fight, I packed my things and my son and went to my aunt Issa's house. My aunt became a big help, she bought KJ diapers without hesitation and she would watch him when I needed her to.

Returned to School for Teen Moms

After I completed my ninth-grade school year I was given a choice by the administrator finish out my entire school year at the center or return to my regular school. I chose to do another year at the pregnancy school. My environment was less stressful at this school because there was less pressure on you as a new mom. I would go between aunt Issa's house and my mom's. I mostly stayed with my aunt however. It saddened me that I had no support from Victor. My mom didn't even want me around, she made a comment about me not stopping her from living her life. I did my best to build a relationship with my mom, but she did not want one. No one taught me how to be a woman, I had to teach myself.

I started to take notice of the white girls. Most were married or engaged. Patricia, my friend, was married. I was jealous a little. I did not have support from my son's father, while other young mothers were going off and getting married.

There was a ten-year-old girl that was pregnant at my school. They moved her forward to the sixth grade so she could attend the school. I felt sorry for her. Who got her pregnant, did anyone think to call the police? No one cared about little Black girls.

Before the school year ended, my Hispanic social studies teacher told me, "Don't lose that beautiful smile of yours." I did not understand what she meant until years later in life. I truly enjoyed her and her classroom, she was very kind to me and the other girls.

My Son's First Birthday

On KJ's first birthday, I did not have extra money to buy him a cake. So, I asked a neighbor friend that was a manager at the grocery store, if he could supply me one. He was happy to do it. I had my son a party that was just me and him. He had a mini pool in the back of our apartment. I asked my little brother to take pictures of me helping him cut the cake. I gave him his first one-dollar bill that day as well. I was hurt that his father didn't make any effort to be there.

No matter what I was going through, I made sure KJ went to every medical check-up, he had food, I taught him manners, and I allowed him to be a child, free of worries.

High school Life Ending

To complete high school, I returned to my old high school for the last two grades. I started working back at Burger World, but at a new location. Life was beginning to look up and stable for me and KJ. I was tired from going to school and work full time, but I made sure me and my son were taken care of.

Victor dropped out of school to play house with Jezebel. I'm glad I never had the thought to drop out.

I was worried about finishing school because I was having trouble passing math. Fortunately, Ms. Harper gave me a little extra help and I was able to pass. With extra credit, I was able to graduate.

Through all the hardship, I was still given recommendations by my teachers for careers. I had a job interview for a professional job in a corporate office and I told my mom about it. She put it in my head that I couldn't do it and I couldn't get the job. I ignored her that time and asked to borrow her car to get to the interview in Miami. When I arrived, all I could do was cry in the car because her voice was repeating in my head. I never went inside.

I knew I was a smart child, but my mom just made me feel like I wasn't smart. I didn't go to my high school graduation because I thought I was fat, didn't look pretty; I earned to walk with my class, but my low self-esteem was at its lowest. When I went the next day to pick up my diploma, I wished I had gone to my graduation, some of my classmates were asking about me. When the school secretary gave a slip that said I ranked 126 out of 330 of my class, I should have been in the lineup to receive my diploma. I worked hard for it, but low self-esteem had power over me. I mean, who wasn't smart? I graduated with a B average with a child.

Not a teacher, school counselor, family member, or friend ever asked me what I want to do after graduation, told me about college, showed me how to open a bank account nothing. No suggestions on how to be a better me or make better decisions.

First Attempt at an Apartment

I wanted my own place and I thought I was ready to live on my own. Doris and I saw some new apartments for rent, that were based on your income, so we applied for a unit.

I was immediately accepted because I was eighteen, but Doris would be eighteen in a month after my moving in. The apartments were newly renovated I was excited I went out and bought bathroom and kitchen supplies. My rent was one hundred thirteen dollars, not bad; I had no furniture, nor could I afford furniture, but I was happy I had done this on my own. I am scared to move in with my son. Afraid of being in this apartment just my son and me. My son and I never slept in this apartment. I paid the first month's rent and did not pay anymore the landlord serve an eviction. I think I would have moved in if Doris had accepted her apartment when she was approved days after her eighteenth birthday, but she chose to back out at the last minute. I didn't want to be in a new space with not knowing anyone.

I packed up my bathroom and kitchen supplies in my mother's car and headed back to her home. Walking back inside my mom's home, she giggled and asked,

"Where are you going?"

"I'm coming back, I don't want to stay there alone," I replied with a slight laugh.

I stayed with my mom a few more months. As I was living with my mom, I took advantage and applied for jobs. I learned when you are fresh out of high school you need a plan, and you need to execute the plan.

I decide I want to go to the military. I always liked the uniform, a former neighbor who was in the military traveled a lot and I wanted to try it. I also wanted better for my son and me. I went to the recruitment office near our home and spoke with the man at the desk. I was ready. I told him I wanted to join the Airforce; he asks me a few questions, the last question he asked is if there are any health issues. I said I have this big tissue on my leg from getting hit by a car. He said I needed to take care of that then come back to see him.

I did just that went to the hospital where my son and I were both born. The doctor looked at the large knot on my leg said we will schedule you an appointment to remove it. I waited for over a month then decided to call the hospital "they said they mailed out the information", I said I did not receive it, the doctor told me the address and it was the wrong address. How could they make such a huge error? I gave up the thought of going into the military. I wrote in my journals several different times that I hate my life.

Get Rid of Me

Now, my mother tells me she is moving; I did not know she was searching for a new apartment or considering moving from this apartment. My mom told me with a laugh that my little brother said,

"If Del is coming to live with us, I am not coming, I will go stay somewhere else."

I went numb. At this time, I was so used to hearing negative words about myself and being mistreated, but I had to move on. I knew my son and I wasn't a problem for anyone, but I could not dwell on that. I went searching for an apartment I had quit Burger World the one stable income I had. But I was tired of working there with no raise in a year and long hours. I also got suspended because my aunt came up there asking me to give her free food and I gave it to her. I knew better, I did it to please her. I was already searching for other jobs, just need more time to get myself a vehicle. I walked by weekly looking at cars at this use car lot sometimes. I would stop in and talk with the owner about any topic everything but me buying a car from him I had no money to buy a car, wishing and hoping I can afford one. Then one day walking to the store I saw a car around the corner from our home for sale. The gentleman selling the car said $500. I thought, "Wow that's cheap…"

I called my dad and asked him for $500 for the car, he wired me $500 within hours. I returned with the money, but the car was sold. It was so disappointing; I knew this was my opportunity to help myself get off to a good start.

I need a job, time's running out for me to move out. I did not think about living with my Aunt Issa again, I didn't like how the neighborhood was going down and I didn't like living there. She was nice and welcoming to us, but I got tired of the back and forth with her. She would pick me up when my mom put me out and drop me back off several months later too much.

New Apartment, No Job

I saw a sign posted at a restaurant: "**HELP WANTED**," next door to the salon that I go to. I ate there a few times and the owners seemed nice. I asked them about the sign on the window and a woman explained,

"Yes, we need help. We are from Germany, and we do not know many people here and we need someone we can trust to open and close the sub shop."

I immediately said yes, I can do it!

The woman, Martha, trained me. The business was slow, she barely made hundred dollars a day. I did not work the 40 hours a week I was accustomed to at Burger World. I was getting a little worried if this lady was going have a difficult time paying me for my time.

I used the $500 my dad gave me to pay on a security deposit and apartment prorated rent. My mother and I are moving out at the same time. My mother gives me a couch, her bedroom set, and I use some of the money buy a cheap dining table for me and KJ. A school friend neighbor helps me move into this new apartment.

After being in the apartment for month things get rocky. The $500 is almost gone and working with Martha is causing tension. She misleads me about how many hours I would work weekly; she gets upset I made one long distance phone call to my mom's job. I needed to ask my mom for a ride somewhere and I had no house phone. This lady tripped over a $2 phone call. She gets so mad, she fires me.

Martha knew I had just moved into a new apartment and had a son, but she did not care. She tricked me with her fake kindness into accepting this job offer.

I asked her for my wages, and she said no. I told her,

"Lady, I need my money I have to pay rent. She still refuses.

I walked over to the cash register and proceed to take my money. She pushes me, I push back, we get to tussling over the register. I was so upset; I used her phone to call my Aunt Donna. I told her what happened while in hysterics. Martha calls the police on me, and they arrive. The police tell her to give me my paycheck and she does. I leave.

This is what after high school life is going to be?

I had to find another job really quick, rent was coming up. I was getting no child support from Victor the system hadn't started garnishing his wages. My Aunt Donna asks me do I want to come down to the Florida Keys with her and her step granddaughter Jenise, to clean rooms at the hotel for one weekend. I agreed. This wasn't a steady job or a job I would have chosen, but I needed the money for rent and to provide for my son. I went to the Florida Keys and left KJ with my Aunt Issa to go clean the hotels rooms.

I did not see any Black people vacating on the beach resort, only white people seem to have the money to vacation here. Cleaning the rooms was awful this is not something I will want to do survive. Cleaning up after white people's hair from the floor and bathtub…this was hard work. After we worked the weekend cleaning rooms. I received my pay of $75 per day. I thought, not bad for a weekend, but this was not enough.

My rent of $375 needed much more than that. Even though I did not like the job, I wanted to return for more pay. My aunt said that was it, then she suggests I go out to eat and shopping. I rode with my aunt and her step granddaughter, so I had no choice but to go. I knew I could not spend any of this money. I tried on one outfit but I did not buy anything like her and Jenise, I felt bad, I needed more clothes but couldn't afford to buy any.

I am back on the job search now. My friend Patricia worked at a retail store and she suggests I put in an application. I did, I was hired days later. Okay know I am thinking maybe I can keep my apartment; I have some stable income. Not three weeks into this new job, I am fired for not having the right clothes on. I did not have professional clothing; I wore the dress I had when I was discharged from the hospital after giving birth to my son. The lady told me why she was letting me go, I had to hold back my tears, and plead for my job. She said no. There was no verbal warning, no written-up warning, the only option was to let me go.

I got on the public transportation to return home. Once there, I sat on my bathroom floor and bawled my eyes out. Crying, asking GOD why?

I decided to move out, I asked the same person who helped me move in to help me move out. I just didn't have no money to pay these bills. My mother did not want all the furniture she gave me because she had brought some new furniture. I knocked on doors and gave the sofa away, the one we had when I lived with my stepfather, it was so hurtful to just give it away I also gave away my brand-new dining table. There was no time to sell anything.

Shoe Man Jack, a Predator

After giving birth to my son KJ, Shoe Man Jack, on two separate occasions, tried to solicit me for sex. I felt uncomfortable around him one day as he was staring at me with this strange look on his face. I was sitting on our chair in the living room watching tv, I got up and left. The first incident my mother was at work, I was tired so I was laying in my mother's bed in her room. Jack comes in the room seat next to me my eyes were closed; they quickly open as soon as I felt a movement in the bed next to me. Jack asks me for sex, whispering. I yelled leave me alone fore I tell momma and the second incident. I wanted to see my mom and her new place I haven't been over there since she moved there. I called my mom at work and say hey I want to stop by she replied' Jack was over there he will let you in I didn't think anything of it. I then rode the public transportation bus. When I arrive Jack buzz me inside the building so I can catch the elevator up. Not fifteen minutes of being at my mom's place in my little brother's room with his door closed. Jack enters and again asking for sex he says "JJ want know", I ran out of my brother's room to the front door and got right back on the public transportation bus headed to my aunt Issa where I was staying. I told my older cousin Shelly what had occurred she only listened gave no advice or comfort. That was the last time I went to the place my mom lived before moving to Atlanta, Georgia.

Back with My Aunt for Last Time

My mom did not volunteer or ask me did I want to come live with her, until I find work. I went back to Burger World but again at a different location, I knew this is the one place I can depend on for income. I worked the five am shift until 1 pm, I had relied on my aunt Issa take my KJ to childcare and my mother to drop me off at work on, her way to work. This arrangement is not what I preferred and this is not how I picture my life. In the afternoon from work I had walk three miles to get back my aunt home because there were no public transportation route in the neighborhood. On my route home was the path of my son's childcare center. The first time I saw my son outside playing in the heat I was upset and to make things worse my aunt had my son in clothes he sleeps in not the clothes I would set out on the table for her to dress him.

I was doing my best to get back on my feet, I applied at the former Burger World I worked at in high school they did give a twenty-cent raise for my return.

My personality was changing to anger, bitterness and aggressive behavior. I was a little girl trapped in a big girl body trying to learn how life works and trying to find my way in the world with a child.

Off to The Unknown

Its time push me further away. I am not bothering anyone, not asking for a handout. I help provide my aunt Issa with a home phone because she did not have one.

My mother had a discussion with her sisters. Leaving her home wasn't good enough, she needs me out of Florida, my aunt Josie called me, conversation sounding all nice, "Josie said you want you come up here to Atlanta, I said "I will think about it" my mother pushing the topic of relocating to Atlanta, Georgia. I called Shelly say 'Hi Shelly Aunt Josie wants me move to Georgia' Shelly said "I don't know Del Aunt Josie money hungry and it's not easy living with them" if you go try it out for two weeks, so if you don't like it you can return". I said OKAY and my friend Yolanda said something similar she" said Del its hard living with family if you have five dollars give them half of it, two dollars fifty cents of it". Both advice was making me nervous about living, but my mom and Josie keep bringing the topic up. Weeks later I told Josie I will come, I put in my two weeks' notice at Burger World paid for a bus ticket months after graduating I am off to Georgia, not you want go college and how can I help you better yourself instead let's get rid of her.

I told my supervisor Peter I was moving to Georgia he said are you sure I said yes, he said "Georgia is too fast for you, you will be back" I just smiled said my goodbyes to my coworkers, I had some amazing coworkers. It was great to see Lester for the last time before I moved to Georgia. I was walking in he gave me a ride; to my job, we did not say much in the car and I did not share I was moving to another state. I called Victor to let him know we were moving away to Atlanta he did not believe me. I told him this is his last time going be able to have easy access to KJ, Victor did not show up last time he heard from us we were in Atlanta, Georgia.

With my son and me, bags mother takes us to the Greyhound bus; we load our things up in one hand my aunt Issa's large blue suitcase and in the other hand my black and white tv my stepfather brought us. I held back my tears waving bye to my mom goodbye. I am off to the unknown. I did not really want to go but from my mom's reaction, she did not want me here in Florida.

Atlanta, Georgia

Here I am in Atlanta, GA when I arrived my first response it's cold and raining in February, I just left sunshine and I have never seen this many black people in one area looks like a riot. I ask my aunt Josie wow so many black people it was a culture shock, where is the white, Asian, and Hispanic people I ask. I saw none on the bus ride to Josie's house. We got off the public transportation Josie had no car, walking down this long road full of large ugly trees to this old beat-up yellow house. It was cold, had no leaves on the trees, looked depressing, old and it was a segregated community except for foreigners that owned the stores. My son and I got settled in our new home; the bedroom was small with a twin bed near the wall. Jane's three children were happy to see us. I wanted to go back home immediately but home to where.

A few weeks in my arrival at my aunt Josie brought a used car, Jane and I began hanging frequently visiting the local parks; I was there for children to play, Jane to look for guys. I soon followed looking for guys, I have no clue what I am doing, I never was a follower I was always a leader, but all that I knew seems to be thrown out the window.

Looking back seems like a setup to destroy me, these are the same people who mentally, physically, and emotionally abused me, why would they want me here with them, as a child, they didn't want me at their home in the summer, so why now?

I see Jane children have no discipline; about three years last time I had seen my little cousin. I was not use to children destroying a home and they did not like clean up and they ate up all the snacks and cereals fast. Jane would buy fourteen boxes of cereal three gallons of milk four days later there would be none for KJ. Keeping food in the house and clean home was not an easy task. Then there was the large dog in the home, with fleas. My appetite change overnight I went from eating too much to eating once a day I wanted make sure my son ate well. My favorite dish became tuna fish sandwich and KJ would eat what Josie had prepared for her children. When she prepared my son plate, I will tell her just give my son a table spoon of everything. I did not want overfeed my son, if he wants more after first serving then he will always ask.

Did not take long for me start getting really depressed, I was alright in Florida working two jobs I knew with guidance and love I could have done better. I can feel a difference in the home beginning to start, my aunt says okay time to look for a job or go to school. I do not even know at this point why I am in Georgia. I am in a new city I have no clue where nothing is. My aunt suggest I apply for food stamps. This what better is in Georgia first thing run government assistance. I did it wasn't much but it helped. I began help buying groceries. I brought groceries on Tuesday then on Thursday all the snacks and juice boxes will be gone, Jane children raid the refrigerator daily. I had nothing to give KJ when he wanted snacks or glass of milk for his cereal. Jane will give the children mix powered milk with water. Next month when I received stamps, I would make sure I put away some snacks in the room for KJ. Jane and Josie didn't like that I explained I do not allow KJ eat up everything in one day, when he wants snacks, I would have some to give him. Jane children will go in my room and steal the snacks. Everything I am trying to teach my son was impossible to do living with Jane and Josie. They made me feel unwanted far too many times. Weeks past I found a restaurant job, I wanted save money so I can move into my own place eight months living in Georgia my mother said KJ can return to visit her in Florida it wasn't help me or because she missed KJ the benefit was given to Shoe man Jack little girl she need a playmate my mother was babysitting his child, but had a problem with my son and me living with her. Shoe man Jack had a little light skin girl, my thoughts on that have always she finally got her light skin daughter. I should have not allowed my son to go, thinking I was doing the right thing. I did not need my son around shoe man Jack, I wasn't thinking. I am always rushing back to my abusers, blocking the hurt. With my son in Florida, I started working another job so by now I have two restaurant jobs, but tension started in my aunt's home. It was never established how much rent I need to give my aunt Josie and what utilities I need to contribute to. I thought she invited me to live with her help me improve-my life. Argument arises it was a problem if I buy myself clothes it's a problem, I rented a bedroom set for KJ and me so we will have a bigger bed and somewhere store our clothes, I was tired of living out of a suitcase, it was a big issue. I began searching for apartment. I did not have much money for an apartment but looking for one making me feel hopeful my situation will soon get better. I did not know any other places to go searching for apartment but up the street from the place Josie was renting, they did not take me round nowhere but to run down areas. Every day I just hope and pray for better. I was lonely and confuse about how to navigate life what to do make life better for myself. Mean time I just sat still trying make the best of a bad situation. Jane meets a man this man has a little brother they introduce me to him. At first, I pay no attention to him. Time passes Josie attitude getting worst toward me but her daughter Jane can do no wrong. I did my best to help out; I grew up in a clean house I would clean the entire house. Jane and Josie will allow Jane three children mess it right back up or allow the dirty flea dog infest with fleas inside the house. I had so many flea bites on my legs by my ankle looked a mess. If it wasn't the fleas, it was the thousands of roaches invading the kitchen, when you turn the light out the roaches will huddle in the middle of the kitchen floor, soon has you turn back on the lights roaches scattered to their neutral corners. Jane and me not hanging around as much. I am seeking another way out and someone to save me and love me. I do not want stay where I am not welcome. I started dating a friend Jane knows, a manipulator that does not work out, then another one I find out he sells drugs I cannot get involved. Jane's boyfriend brother wants to get to know me more I say okay. I was wanting somebody to be kind to me and feel loved. We start dating right away. This boy was immature I did not care, I now have somebody to talk, share my time and keep me company. The sexual, emotionally abuse can take a toll on your outlook on how you view your body, makes you feel like in order to feel love you must lay down with the person away without much thought in turn to poor decision. When I came to Georgia I had lots of gold jewelry, rings, necklaces, between Jane and Tom I believe one of them stole it, I discovered Tom stole my food stamps, few cash and my food stamp card that I use to pick up my stamps. Jane's son stole seventy dollars from me I notice that immediately when I was looking through my money stash along with some jewelry. Over time before my daughter was born, I had none of the jewelry it was slowly disappearing. Several months past I think I might be pregnant I tell Jane she smirks. I did not tell anyone else I am possible pregnant not even Tom. While mostly going with limited interaction with Josie and Jane because I am getting the silent treatment again. I did my best stay out of Jane and Josie way at home. I was still working two jobs, every day after work I would stop at this Chinese restaurant for dinner so I would not need to use Josie kitchen. I love local Chinese restaurant braised chicken wings first time ever having this flavor wings. I visit the place so much the owner started giving me free wings occasionally. I was spending a lot of time with Tom at his mom's place or at the park so I wouldn't have to be at my aunt's home much. At times when I would return from my aunt's place, she, Jane and her children will be gone but the door will be unlocked for me to get in. I would wonder where they went, no note was left of their whereabouts house would be dark. I did not know where they had gone, then my cousin Shelly would call me ask why I hadn't come down Dublin with Jane and Josie, my response they never said they were going there and nor did they ask me. Josie and Jane will stay in Dublin for a week never call to check on me. I told Shelly you were right Josie hungry for money, and they are mistreating me. More tension rises, Tom is no longer allowed to visit me at my aunt house I think because Jane was having problems with Tom's brother. Tom and me would stay far away from my aunt house when he visited. Everyday my aunt act as if I'm invisible, my aunt order forty boxes of braised chicken wings, she would not offer me not one box of the wings, everyone including Jane children was eating in front of me like I did not exist. They seem to be jealous if I did anything for myself. Josie will allow her daughter Jane take her money and buy expensive shoes for herself but before I started working two jobs, I would have to give Josie eighty dollars from two hundred thirty-five dollars of my welfare check. Things were getting worst I returned the rental bedroom set the attitude toward me because I am renting a nice bedroom set for my son and me have something decent. Josie felt like I should begiving her that money instead. My aunt did not have the nice furniture I grew up with nice clean furniture everything at her house was highly used and damaged. Now my cousin Robert from Dublin Georgia comes to live with us, while he works in downtown on construction project. He was cool to talk to but he kept his distance he notices the hostility toward me. The first week of Robert living with us and Tom comes to visit me, we stayed outside for about one hour talking, then he leaves, I returned inside my aunt home seating in the hall way folding clothes, my aunt said something under her breath, she quickly gets up and strike me with the heel of a shoe in the temple of my forehead, I screamed so loud Tom ran back inside the house trying to defend me. I was screaming what did I do she could never say what I did or gave me an apology. I started searching for a new place to live, then a coworker said I can come live with her and her husband. Leaving, I pack my bags while Josie and Jane visit Dublin, they have no idea where I had gone. I then get in touch with my mom she tells me come and get KJ. I leave for Florida, when I arrive Victor comes to visit, he has no idea I may be pregnant, my mom gets upset when Victor and me go outside to talk. I need Victor to save me and help me. Nobody could have told me Victor and me would not be together for life. Victor asks me if I am alright, I went ahead without much to tell him things are not better in Georgia.

He was the only person I had ever wanted to be with, it wasn't puppy love for me as people would say. Victor had issues at home as well, but still was no excuse to neglect our son and me. I return back to Georgia I know my mom was thrilled; she didn't want me back in Florida. The new living arrangement did not last very long before Risa trick me into giving her twenty dollars until pay day and her husband called me in their room asking me for sex when she was at work. I lived with Risa two more weeks after her husband made advances toward me, I never told Risa why I had shortened my stay I did not want to cause no problems in a woman's home.

After returning from Florida, the new manager at Ms. Autumn's judged me for being pregnant and not married. He was a pastor. I went from working a small number of hours to no hours because he took me off the schedule. Now I have no job while living with Risa for two more weeks. I need a new place to go.

Homeless Pregnant
and More Abuse

It was time to go but where, I reach out to my dad for help and money. He suggests that I ask my aunt can I move back in with her; the next day I asked my aunt can I come back, and I will give her $150 for rent. Several weeks living back with my aunt my mother tells me Jane and Josie are moving from the house in a few months I ask where they are going, she said she did not know. I could only think why Josie would take my money knowing, I will have nowhere to go. My mother did not offer me to come live with her, I did not ask. I did not ask Josie or Jane when they were moving. I keep living with them praying for better.

Then on top of getting me homeless months later Tom becomes physically and verbally abusive. I subject my son and myself to domestic violence. Toms pull a gun out on me, hits me in the head while walking with my son down the street. I ran for help at a stranger's house. I had no power in me to fight and get away from these types of people. I went from bad to worse, all my relationships with people involves physical, emotional and mental abuse. Later in life I found out Tom's mother was in an abusive relationship with his father. Life has a way of repeating itself. Every day I was living to do my best to find joy within myself and provide a happy childhood much as possible for my son.

I told myself have to get away from these people, I couldn't work much as before I was so sick during this pregnancy my prenatal care was limited, I was too sick to take the public transportation to work or to the doctor for my to the doctor for my checkups and more stress and my working hours was not enough to afford rent. My aunt had a car never offered me a ride to the doctor. I started calling around to different daycare centers inquiring about work Mr. Brooks a local daycare owner was such a blessing for me, he hired me over the phone. He said I need someone to ride the van bus for two weeks with me I will pay you cash of two hundred dollars. I made sure to spend the money slow and wisely. Weeks later during another phone call my mom says Josie leaving Georgia I ask where's Jane going she does not know. Everyone having this discussion without telling me anything. My mom suggests I ask Jane can I live with her. I ask Jane can I come with her when she moves. I told her I would give her $150 a month. Fortunately, she agreed.

"Too many women in my life and in my community will talk about you, look down on you, hate on young girls just to make themselves feel better. They do not understand that a mature woman with self confidence in herself and walking in peace teaches and uplifts." Titus 2:3-5, Matthew Chapter 7: 1-5

My son and I move in and the environment is still hostile. I did my best to keep us out of Jane's way. I paid her 3 months' rent for a bedroom with a pad on the floor. It was fine for us since we were not homeless. I was trying to have a safe place to go after delivering my daughter, who is coming soon. Giving Jane her rent money left me with only $85 a month until my next rent check.

In July my mother gave birth to a daughter with Jack. August I delivered a beautiful little girl. No one came to visit me in the hospital, I almost lost my daughter from a lack of oxygen, but me and her made it through.

Home from the hospital after delivering my daughter, my aunt Josie, gave me a bag with used baby clothes that someone had given her. I really appreciated it, Tom brought a box of diapers and never brought anything after that. His mother, Ms. Tout, tells me he was disappointed it was a girl because he wanted a boy. The nerve of people. I didn't even entertain her comment. In my mind as a woman and mother, Ms. Tout should have corrected her son.

Homeless With a Newborn Baby

Living with Jane was just like living with her mom, except for the rowdy and messy children. They would eat up all the groceries, never keep the house clean and I would clean it up. I would not say anything because it is their mother's house. I need a place for me and my children to live. I would babysit Jane's first child for free, long before I had kids. Jane and her children would hurt me by leaving KJ behind when it was time to wake up for school in the morning. When it was time to wash clothes, Jane had a car and would not load my children's things. Instead, I would have to walk in the cold with 8-week-old daughter. I had no money to buy my daughter diapers, so I used cloth diapers. I had 10, when one got wet, I would hand wash it and hang it up to dry.

I had to return to work, although I did need new glasses or contacts just to see the menu on the board. My supervisor said I could return. I had a babysitter lined up and she was willing to watch my children until I received my first paycheck. I asked Jane if I could hold off on paying rent for October so I could purchase some glasses and get my hair done to look presentable at work. I explained to her that I would make more money than the $200 a month I was receiving from government assistance and that I could give her more each month.

Jane agreed to these terms at first. October came and I didn't actually receive my government assistance check. I called the office and the worker said they mailed it, although I did not receive it.

I realized I had not alerted the government of my address change before they mailed the check. I went back to the old residence, hoping to find it there or by waiting on the mail carrier.

When I arrived, there was no hope. The mail carrier did not have anything and there wasn't anything in the mailbox addressed to me. I was stressed because the job was not giving me many hours to work and the babysitter could not watch my children on the weekend.

I had a suspicious feeling that Jane and aunt Josie may have stolen my check. Back then, you could cash anyone's check without showing ID if the clerk recognized you. I went to the welfare office and updated my address. I did not want to tell Jane that I had no money to give her for October rent. I was hoping the office would resend the check if it hadn't been cashed yet. I waited and there was no check for October or November in 1991.

The living arrangement with Jane was miserable. She made it very clear that my children and I were not welcome anymore. Her boyfriend who provided no assistance whatsoever got to stay there, however as she pampered him and fed him for free.

I did not know when I would receive any income. I did receive food stamps so I was able to feed my family. By the grace of GOD, I got a call from the IRS. They would be sending me a check for $1,600 for unpaid child support by Victor. Upon receiving the check in her mailbox, my mother asked me for

$300 of it. I told her she could have it. I love my mother and I'm always looking out for others before myself. My mother sent me the cashier's check the second week of November and I waited for over a week.

I confronted my mom asking her why the check hasn't arrived. She claims I should have gotten it by now. My mother returned to the bank and she was informed that someone tried to cash the check. That someone was Jane.

I had to wait 30 days before the bank would issue another cashier's check. I held onto Jane's mailbox key until my check arrived. My check arrives a few days before Thanksgiving and the last week of school for my son before a holiday break.

Tony arrives for the holiday to visit Jane. Jane decides to leave me a note detailing how she wants me and my children to get out of her house immediately. I decided to discuss this matter in person, like adults.

"Why are you kicking me out? I just got my check and I can give you some money. I don't see you getting mad at the men you allow to live here for free."

Jane starts hitting and I fight her back. After we cooled down, I called my mom and told her the sad news. She said I should leave and come back to Florida. I told her,

"If I can't make it here, I can't make it anywhere."

In the back of my head, I'm also thinking about how my mother treated me when I lived with her. I know it won't be much better if I run away to Florida. I know I would be thrown out and made to stay with my aunt Issa once again to make room for Shoe Man Jack and his family.

I packed my and my children's belongings and picked KJ up from school. It was a cold day in Georgia. Tony asked me where I was going and I told him to a hotel. He asked if I had money and I simply showed him what was left of the cashier's check.

I loaded us all into a cab and he asked, "where to?"

I told him to go to the nearest hotel. I did not know where else to go.

I haven't explored Atlanta; Georgia like I would have liked to. I have only been introduced to the poverty and toxic side of it all.

When we arrive at the hotel, the concierge asks how long we will be staying. Unsure, I just say a week.

Our room had a tv, a nice bed, and a warm shower. I had to warm my daughter's bottle up in the sink, but we were safe together. All of KJ and my meals came from a local restaurant.

I did not want to focus on my problems any longer. It was Thanksgiving and my family was spending it in a hotel. I called Ms. Tout looking for Tom. She and I start catching up and I tell her that the kids and I are living in a hotel. She then invites us over for Thanksgiving dinner. After getting off the phone with Ms. Tout, I felt like everything will be just fine. I appreciated her kindness deeply and to my surprise, Tom decided to join us. It was a happy Thanksgiving, and for that, I am very thankful.

That same Thanksgiving Day in 1991, I made the decision to work towards getting my family a car. The following week, I loaded up my children on the bus and went to a few car dealerships I knew of in aunt Josie's neighborhood. I was determined to drive off someone's car lot with a car of my own.

I eventually found the perfect car and the only car I could afford. It was a 1986 Buick Skylar for $300 down and $160 a month. I drove off the lot without any car insurance or car seats for my kids. My next stop was a retail store to buy car seats.

I was happy, but money was getting low. I was starting to regret giving my mom that $300.

I didn't know where else to turn so I turned to Ms. Tout. I explained that money was low and with the car and hotel expenses, I didn't know how long I could keep my head above water. I didn't think she would be so generous as to offer us a place to stay. I finally felt a little relief after she said that.

I did not take advantage of her kindness or get too comfortable while living with Ms. Tout and Tom. I did not have any money to give her, but I paid my dues by giving her home a deep cleansing and buying groceries for the house with my food stamps. I began looking for an apartment for the kids and me. The part-time job I had would barely cover rent, but I needed a place for us.

In December, I called the welfare office to see if they mailed out this month's check. They informed me that they did and that it should have arrived by now. I went to see Jane and check if it was in her mailbox.

When I get there, Jane knows just what I am talking about and tells her daughter *not* to give me my check. My aunt Josie and brother Tony are sitting around, watching this happen, mouths zipped shut. I went to the public phone and proceeded to call the police. That put some fire under her because she gave me my check before I could finish my call.

I felt like they were jealous because I drove up in a car that I got all on my own. Satan always has a plan, but GOD is always in control. These people, who were supposed to be my family, wanted to destroy me. I was very disappointed by my older brother's actions or lack thereof. Had the roles been switched, there would be no catching a cab or bus to go live in a hotel. I always defended and helped my brothers whenever they needed it.

My daughter's first Christmas came. I was depressed and missed my mom. I didn't have any family around for the holidays and no money to buy kids gifts. No one calls to find out how we are doing or where we are living. I was grateful that Ms. Tout opened her doors to us, but not having any money during Christmas was disheartening.

Tom was no help either. He was getting meaner and meaner as things slowly looked up for me and the kids. He was also triggered by Ms. Tout and my bonding as she gave me life advice and was looking out for me. This is something I have very rarely had in my life.

I liked Ms. Tout quite a bit. She carried herself well; the lady was always dressed well, she spoke well and was kind-hearted. She wasn't your timid grandmother with cookies and pies, she was sophisticated. I needed a figure like this in my life right now.

KJ returned to school, which was in Jane's neighborhood. I did not want to uproot him from his school, he needed some stability. I enrolled

I learned then that when people see you struggling or trying to make it if they not happy within themselves, they will go out their way to make your life hell.

him in the after-school program to give him even more positive activities. It was $5 a week. The school did a great job, they helped him with his homework, gave them fun games to play, and sometimes gave them hot meals. I was fortunate to have found a babysitter for my daughter right before Jane put us out.

Going back and forth from Ms. Tout's home to Jane's neighborhood was difficult. KJ attended school there and the babysitter for my daughter lived there. I borrowed gas money from Ms. Tout because I was barely working 25 hours per week. This was not by choice, the manager, Robin, was not a very good boss at all. I would hear things from other employees after I left work of her gossiping about me. When it was slow at work, I would be her first choice to cut for the day, after having worked only 4 hours. I figured she was jealous of me since she was talking bad about me and sending me home early. She said nothing to my face of course.

I never asked Tom why he wasn't working and his mother never pushed him to get a job. As time went on, I met Tom's dad. He told Tom he needed a job to provide for his family, thereafter he began to work for his father's lawn care business.

School is now over for my son. The lady that watched my daughter agreed to watch KJ for the summer. I had to pay her $65 a week for this service. I was working, a small number of hours, to pay for childcare and

GOD is still working on me. I always cried out to him to help me please stop making the same mistakes. As a child, at the age of 11, I asked GOD to use me...I asked, is this is it...I have no idea.

car payments. I could not afford car insurance so I had none. I went searching for a summer camp for KJ and my first stop was a church.

Amazingly, I found a nice Black woman to help me with summer camp. There weren't many children at the camp, but it did not bother KJ or me. It was $15 a week with meals so I was grateful. I told Tom he needed to babysit his daughter so I can work. I was taking care of three kids at this point.

I decided to return to the babysitter for my daughter. She was a Jehovah's Witness and I was bragging about the church summer camp I found for KJ to her. Her daughter looked up at me with a smile, while the babysitter frowned. I let her know I get paid this upcoming Wednesday and I would be back to pay her. I paid her frown no mind.

I learned from KJ that the babysitter had been hitting my daughter and being mean to her, so she wasn't getting any more of my money.

My First Apartment in Atlanta, Georgia

Going to live with Ms. Tout, I did not get comfortable. She helped me a lot by lending me money for gas and I always paid her back on time. She never did ask me for the money back though.

January of 1992, my infant daughter and I went searching for an apartment. The first unit, a lady Ms. Jeanette shows me is a one-bedroom unit. It's going for $295; I thought maybe I could afford this. After touring it, I was no longer interested considering its condition. The unit was all the way in the back of a long hallway, which was dirty and it just looked scary. I couldn't let my kids live in this dump and I told her that.

The next day, Ms. Jeanette calls me at Ms. Tout's home saying she had another unit for me to see. It was quite nice and looked more expensive.

I asked her how much it would be,

"Don't tell anyone, but we have your name at the top of the list for a new housing assistance program." She replied.

I was incredibly happy; it was a nice apartment. There were bullet holes on the front door and drug users would sit on the stairway. Thankfully, they would leave when we arrived and they never messed with us. I did not allow Tom to move in with us.

For a little while, my children and I slept on the floor. It did not bother me because it was my own home. Ms. Tout gave me a number to a place giving out free furniture for homes. My home was peaceful. I was getting back on my feet, doing better, making better choices, and just doing my best to get back on track.

I registered for school to be a Medical Assistant. I became an honor roll student while working full-time. I couldn't be happier; I have a car and a safe home for my children and me.

Tom started helping to watch our daughter and helping in the evening watching my son while I went to night school. My school offered childcare, but sometimes it was difficult picking the kids up from school and bringing them to mine.

My work schedule was 6 AM to 2 PM, Monday-Friday. On Fridays, there were no classes.

Tom started out fine watching the kids. Then he started coming for just two days a week, then no days. He would be more willing to babysit when I brought the kids to his home, but eventually, he wouldn't answer the door at all. I had to bring them to school with me.

Tom was not the best babysitter anyway; he would eat my children's food I packed. He also stole my daughter's earrings and put them in his own ears.

I was no longer working 40 hours; we had new management at Ms. Autumn's restaurant. For some reason, in my experience, Black managers abuse their power by shitting on people.

Jane and her children ended up moving into the same building as us. Jane never comes to visit us, however. She would send her children to borrow dish or laundry detergent. I did not like that because if I didn't have those things in my home, I had to just go without. I had nothing extra to give to anyone. I am learning to budget to stay afloat. I watched my aunt Issa budget every week, laying out all her expenses on the table. She would sit for hours budgeting the little money she had.

Life was going well, it was hard, but it was good. That is until I lost my car after having it for only a year. I was tired of paying the car payment and the repo man came to collect at my job, cold. I tried to get the car back, but in order to get it back, I had to pay the two months payment I had missed and the repo man. I told them to keep it. Big mistake.

I missed my car as me and my children had to walk and take public transportation everywhere. I was so disappointed in myself. I am back walking in the cold with my two babies. Tom would come over to babysit occasionally, he's working a lot for his dad's business.

I learned from my mom that Jane moved from the apartment building we shared. She was gone for several months before I found out. I was hoping to develop a better relationship with her since I did not have much family here.

My Daughter's Second Christmas

I was home with my children with no money to go home to Florida, not that anyone invited us to come anyway. We were watching movies and enjoying each other. I cooked a small holiday dinner. Grace, a friend from work, was walking me through how to make my first Christmas meals and my first pan of chicken dressing.

Later in the afternoon, I learned that my daughter did not have any more diapers so my two kids and I caught the bus in the cold to go get some.

My mother told me where Josie and Jane had moved and she felt the need to tell me they had two vehicles. I stopped by their home on the way from the store, which was closed for Christmas, so a waste of a trip.

My children and I walked across the railroad track to where my cousin and aunt lived. I saw the two vehicles Josie had parked in front of her building. I knocked on the door and Jane did not greet me with a warm welcome, but she did allow us to come in. The environment was tense.

Jane and Josie cooked a large holiday meal for their family. My aunt knows I like her chicken casserole, but offered me none, or my children any food for that matter. Josie was on the telephone with my mother. She gave me the phone and I spoke with my mom briefly; she was not talking about anything important. Her conversation had a very sarcastic tone.

I said to her, hurt,

"When I get on my feet, I am not doing nothing for nobody."

She chuckled. I said that because the treatment from my family was horrible.

When I left their house, I knew the buses ran on a holiday schedule. Therefore, one bus every two hours. My cousin nor my aunt did offer my small family a ride home. I walked two miles home with my kids. I was so hurt. My children and I walking, alone, on Christmas Day in the cold. My eyes were tearing up, it made no sense to me. How could they be so nasty to me?

My mom never addresses these people about what they've done to me. This was nothing new. I am not used to people coming to my defense, I have fought my own battles.

Another Car with Abuse

My aunt Josie reached out to me months later about a car auction. She explained that her friend Nikki, along with her husband Walter, could take me to the auction to get a good car for less than $500. My aunt dropped me off to these crazy people.

We all loaded up in Walter's car to go to the auction. I am thinking, "nice of these people to help me find a good cheap car."

The car was an ugly car, but I didn't mind, I needed something. Walter tells me to drive it to their home because the car kept cutting off. While he's looking under the hood of the car, we're laughing about the situation.

Nikki tells her daughter, Claire, that I was flirting with her husband. His stepdaughter rushes up, yelling at me. I'm confused by her actions; my children are here and she's way bigger than me. She starts pushing me while cursing at me. I couldn't do anything but cry.

I told Walter to give me the keys, I will try to make it home by myself. While driving home, the car cuts off about 20 times before I could reach home. On the last cut off, the police roll up to us. He tells me I need to get the car out of the road. I explain the situation to him and that I need a push. He refuses to help me but tells me I need to get it out of the road.

I started it up one last time while hitting the gas hard, fortunately, it stayed on to get us home. Months later I sold the car to my aunt Josie for $300.

Come income tax time, I'm looking for a new vehicle. I paid Josie and Jane to take me to the dealership. They dropped me off and left. I was able to get a 1993 Ford Escort. The down payment was $3,500, which was a total rip off. The car let me down far too many times for that kind of money.

Tom did not help with the finances much. He acted as if I owed him a good life. I kept him around as a free babysitter, but I knew he was jealous of me. He thought I was supposed to provide for him as well.

One day, his jealousy got the best of him. Tom busted out the window of my car with his foot while sitting on the passenger side. He did this because I wouldn't buy him a steak biscuit. Another time he knocked down my TV after I told him to get out of my house acting crazy.

When he destroyed my stuff, I took the VCR he gave me and threw it out the hall window, almost striking him in the head. I went back out and tried to pick up the pieces of the VCR. Tom and I went our separate ways.

I did have to locate him for child support. He lied to the judge saying he was mentally ill and could not pay. Fortunately, the judge did not go for his lies. Now it was just me and my children once again. I had a serious problem with abusive people. Thus far, almost everyone I've encountered has been overly disrespectful or abusive. I could not allow my children to see their mother abused.

Toxic Live and Abuse

Grace is the same age as my mom. I met her around the same time I met David. Grace warned me, "Del baby, that boy is crazy, you need to let him alone." I did not want to listen.

I met someone else when my daughter was two and my son seven. This mans who had just started working at the restaurant, Ms. Autumn's with me in the evening during a double shift. He seemed like a nice and good person. He's handsome and has two jobs. I told myself, my next relationship, if there's any signs of abuse in the first two months, that is not the one and I am out.

I was taking better care of me. I lost weight, I was looking and feeling good. My children got to be children and were thriving. I even have a house phone and I keep my hair and nails done. Ms. Tout had warned me once, "When you let a man in your home, it's hard to get that negro out. He thinks he owns your shit."

David and I started dating and things were going pleasantly well. One day when I was going to take my children to the park, I had on a nice yellow outfit. This fool rips my shirt off of me. As time passes and we're doing more family stuff, he asks me to marry him. I said yes. I am in love and going to get married so what do I do, I have my third child in 1994. I did not need David, but I kept telling myself that I love him, and he loves me.

Grace was there through it all with encouraging words to leave that crazy fool. Abuse is again what I have to deal with. Domestic violence is what I saw my aunt go through and what Victor's mom went through. A friend of mine, Joy, had it bad. Her husband stabbed her so bad she ran to my home for help. It's sad. Black women have endured so much pain by our black males, families, and society. It does not help when Black women baby their boys, cater to the boy's or adult son's needs while hindering their growth. Making excuses for their toxic behavior. That's all Girthy ever did with David. I am starting to see a pattern with me. Victor's mom, Tom's mom, and David's mom.

In May of 1996, I finally pressed charges and not before feeling this little girl is not nobody burnt trash. I had enough of people putting their hands on me. I was an adult, but the little girl inside of me was crying for help.

David and His Mom Not Right

A few incidents that stand out before May 1996 is one when he hits me in my head with an ashtray in front of my four-year-old daughter. He hit me in the eye, leaving it black and bruised. He even pulled a knife on me when I was pregnant and again, I stayed with the abuser. Girthy and me get into a fist fight at the hotel she was living, at the time. All because she said I was acting funny.

Girthy was verbally abusive, she would always defend David's toxic behavior when speaking to me. If I tell her to stop babying him, she would always counter with,

"That's my child, my baby. He doesn't need nobody."

She once had David steal my phonebook with all of my contacts. She reported me to Family Children Services. Not because my children were in danger, it was to be toxic and hurtful towards me. If she reads this book, she will find out I knew it was her, but I still chose to be around her and be kind to her.

Girthy invited me and my children to her home for Memorial Day, 1996. I didn't have a car because my Ford Escort needed a new transmission which was over $2,000 for the part and the labor. I should have known not to go over there, but I always want to be around family and feel wanted and accepted.

The time we spent together was fine up until the end. When we were leaving her home to catch the bus, I was hoping one of her relatives would offer us a ride home since I only lived three miles away. Girthy didn't drive in the dark so she wasn't an option. I was leaving because David started to get emotionally and physically abusive.

"Stop acting crazy, David. You're embarrassing yourself," I told him in an agitated tone.

He gets up and twists my arm to the point where I think he's going to break it. He's doing this while I am holding our barely two-year-old son. None of his family members helped me. I walked to a neighbor's house across the street to call the police and my cousin Jane to pick me up. I pressed charges on David. He was ordered to take an anger management class and did probation for a year. I did get back with David and after the years of failed marriage engagements, I finally let him alone. I kept putting myself and my children in a position to be abused and to witness an unhealthy relationship.

In 1997, I went to get another car. This car was much nicer than all the rest. David was still popping in and out of my life and he was jealous of this new ride. He was also jealous of the close relationship KJ and I had with each other.

KJ was getting older, and I could trust him to watch his younger siblings. One day, I was gone longer than I expected when picking up the new vehicle. When I arrived home, David and the police pulled up as well. David called the police in hopes of getting me locked up for leaving my kids home alone. I had to act fast. I asked my neighbor that lived downstairs to say she was watching my children.

Fortunately, the police bought the story. I walked upstairs where my children were waiting for me and got on my knees thanking GOD for this new car and for his GRACE. I took my babies in our new car to go eat out that night. I told David to kiss my black ass as we left. I kept going back to him, it was like a drug addiction.

During a phone conversation with Girthy, she confided in me that David's dad's mom would treat her like crap. I had to ask if that is why she's so nasty to me. It was crickets on the phone. It explained why Girthy carried such pain and project-ed on to others. But at what age do you seek to learn and grow from the past. You must put in the effort and change the toxic pattern.

I began to see myself different-ly. I start to realize I do not need these guys. They did not know how to be independent. Their mommas spoiled them. They had no car when I met them and didn't know anything about fixing one up. I taught myself by watching me-chanics. I even had to teach David how to change a tire and how to install a water hose on a car. He never volunteered to wash my car or fill up the tank. I had to do it all, while pregnant at that some-times. Neither one of them (Tom or David) had an apartment of their own.

Devil gets busy and the little lonely girl in me wants to feel accepted and loved. Poor and irrational choices lead me to unstable environments. It led to multiple moves with my children to different places. I felt like I wanted or needed more.

I was supporting myself and my children on my own. They were just a bag of trash, a babysitter sometimes. I was carrying around the assumption that an adult male will fix me and make me better, but I was already better doing it all on my own. No matter how hard times got for me, I never went back to Florida, and I was never homeless again. I made sure of that. My children would not be homeless, and no one could ever put us out.

I let David go completely in 1999. I gave him 30 days' notice to get out of my house. I could not take it no more, a man sitting around with no business about himself. When I put David out of my home, it felt so good. This time, I did not allow him back in my life. I bought all new furniture to further cleanse my home. My children were happier, I went back to school, and I was focusing on more positive things. I also didn't have to deal with his mom...Double blessing.

Holidays, Celebrate If I Want

Holidays were very painful for me in Atlanta. It was very painful not having the extra money to buy things for my children and it was very painful not being around family.

I would attend the free toys drive for low-income community members to get free gifts for my kids. It was mostly Black women who stood in the long line for hours. This felt like the most humiliating thing, walking in line with a large black bag to get free toys for your children. Just so they would have something under the tree.

During the holidays my family would gather in Florida, but I had no money to attend. One relative who will remain unnamed, got everyone together for a Christmas trip and did not want me to attend. No one shared the details until after it was over. I should not have felt lonely during the holidays. My bills were paid and we had food, but the little girl inside me wanted to be accepted with a big family and a good feast.

As I started learning more about history, I began to understand more of where I belong in this world. Holidays and the tie to religion is manmade and they are not created equally. People in a certain tax bracket, Christmas and Thanksgiving can bring great depression and loneliness. People such as myself having to ask for free toys for my children instead of my focus on what we did have.

We were told Jesus is a blue-eyed blonde, white man for far too long. When the Bible describes HIM as having hair like wool and feet burnt as brass, it sounds Black to me. I will not allow myself to be misled by false teachings. Thanksgiving is not celebrated by Native Americans; it is actually a slap in their face and their culture. Holidays for me now, are just for beautiful decorations and family time, if I choose to celebrate.

Attending Church with Children

Church was a safe place. A place I felt good and was moved by the spirit. I wanted my children to know when times get difficult, they can always call on GOD. I told them to always put GOD first in their lives. I visited several local churches when my kids were all under twelve, we never joined until years later. The stares you get at certain churches, as a young single Black mother, were unwelcoming to say the least. I kept going despite the stares. At one church, I walked up to shake the pastor's hand and his wife gave me the dirtiest look. I never returned to that one after that.

The thing I wanted to do the most in church was join the choir. Being told you cannot sing is the reason my confidence fell short for me trying to join. Something about singing or hearing someone sing hymns…it moves my soul. It is a cleansing feeling. I do not like feeling disconnected from GOD. If I do, it means I am not giving HIM enough of me.

Love Me

I was seeking love in all the wrong places. I never felt safe with adults. I love others who choose to not love me back. I forgave others because I will not allow Satan to steal my joy. If I want GOD to forgive me for my sins, I must forgive my sister and brother. Those who abused me and hoped I would fail; well, I continue to thrive and be great. HIS blessing over my life has been my haven. I am beautiful because I am made in HIS image. The world did give this life, this joy and this peace and the world shall not taketh it away.

I focus on What I Did Right as a Young Mother

I was a young mother carrying a huge bag of hurt, pain, and abuse. I gave my children love. I am most proud of myself as a mother I introduced my children to GOD. I did not make excuses. I did not use and abuse drugs or go out clubbing. I drank maybe twice a year. I was involved in my children's education as much as I was able to be. I did not throw my children off on others. I was always willing to learn better for myself and my children. I made sure my children remained in good health with yearly doctor and dental visits. I taught my children life skills, including but not limited to, opening a checking and savings account, how to maintain how to maintain good credit, how to apply for college, be a good citizen etc.

Everything was not always done right; I can admit that. But it was done to the best of my abilities and knowledge at the time. I can sleep well knowing I did my best and gave it my all. I walked in a straight line as much as possible. I stay praying and doing my best to be faithful to GOD. I did not want HIM to take me away from children and have someone else raise them. GOD answered all my prayers. I am still here; I saw my children grow into responsible adults. I now get to enjoy my beautiful granddaughters and not watching them struggle. GOD'S love, my faith, favor, and mercy over my life. I am so blessed to be a grandmother filled with laughter and give my granddaughters so much positive love and continue living my best LIFE.

Dedication to My Daughter

I love you dearly. You know I make no excuse, I blame no one. Our relationship suffered because of my poor relationship with women. My hurtful childhood carried into my motherhood. You're hurt by me; we clashed so many times. You suffered because I thought I was protecting you, but I did not protect from sexual abuse. If I had dealt with my issues before giving birth to you, maybe you wouldn't have too many issues of your own to deal with now. Me needing to feel loved by family and in their presence, put you in the presence of a monster. Jane's son, Sammy, would have never been able to molest you then, in the pool. I am so sorry for that. I always wanted to be accepted by my family, but not at the expense of hurting my daughter. If I knew how to make better choices in my life, this would have never happened. If I loved myself more, this would have never happened. I know you have forgiven me, and I have forgiven myself, but you are my everything, Chocolate Chip. Continue to be great and do not allow anyone to steal your joy.

Whole Different Life Experience

I know I am a good person despite what others have said or how others want to portray me. I am worthy of love; I knew this time will be different if I decide to allow someone into our lives because I was different. Someone told me it was something in me that kept attracting these kinds of men. I started searching deep within myself and within my life to break this cycle. I had graduated from medical assistant school, and I was advancing more personally and professionally.

I visited Grace's house who had a six-year-old granddaughter. That baby had an old spirit and an insight like no other. She said,

"Del, your husband's coming. You're going to have twins."

This was funny coming from this little girl. I had been Praying for a GOD-fearing man who wants to grow old together. A man who is not selfish and who wants to share wonderful experiences together.

I was grateful to have my stepfather for seven years. He was good to my mom and to me and my siblings. I wanted my children to witness their mom in the same kind of healthy relationship. I also wanted my boys to see what a responsible man was supposed to do.

I started working this new job in the gardening department. One day in the break room, I saw these two tall dark skin men talking. They were loud, but one was louder. He was laughing so loud. I was thinking to myself, I wish he would hush up. I saw that loud man again weeks later. We did not talk, just walked past each other. I realized he worked at the same company and was not just a vendor like the other guy he was with weeks ago.

Months went by and I did not see him again until June of 2006. Once again, we were walking by each other, but this time he stopped in front of me. We started talking and he seemed nervous while holding this conversation. I was thinking…is this man flirting with me?

My new rules. 1. Do not date a man with children under ten. There's always drama with the momma. 2. I am not raising nobody's children. Nobody helped me raise mine. I did not follow my own new rules. I have been more detailed when I prayed for a God-fearing husband.

I asked him if he was married and he starts rambling about how he's getting divorced because his wife cheated on him. Apparently, she contracted an STD and he was glad they had stopped sleeping together long before that. I told him I thought that was terrible, but he would learn and grow from the situation. I walked away and returned to work. I did not expect all that from him and I did not expect him to be so nice. I guess he needed a listening ear that day.

I ran into him again the following month. Now I'm working as a cashier and he walks by. I learn his name is Vidal. We start a conversation along with another coworker. Vidal is much quieter now. He says he's celebrating the 4th at his sister's house. I told him to bring me a plate as a joke.

I told him about some of the places I visit in Atlanta, in particular, a place on the westside I take my boys to get their hair cut. He said he knew the spot and that he, "needed to roll with me one day." I said sure, give me your phone number. I wasn't thinking too into it besides coworkers hanging out. I told him he had good handwriting and that it made mine look terrible. We laughed together.

As time goes on, Vidal and I talk more. We're both cashiers so we see each other more often. He shows me a burn on his forehead from working on his car. He tells me he works two jobs. I touched his belly and said, "I need to holla at you." He replied, "you can." Our supervisor was looking at us while smiling. Weeks went by before I gave him a call inviting him to go out. He said yes, he just needed to put his boys to bed.

My thoughts were centering on just mingling with another adult, making a friend and nothing else.

There's a saying that children are a packaged deal with a significant other. After my experience, I say it is not a packaged deal if you did not give birth to the kids or you did not adopt them. If the other parent is still living, it is not your responsibility to do anything but support your spouse. People need to stop telling stepmothers it is their responsibility to nurture someone else's children. If they choose to, that is fine, but men are not held to that same standard. The stepmother's job is to support the father, be kind to the child, but not full out raise them.

When he said, "boys," plural, I knew I did not want to be nobody's stepmother. Been there, done that.

Vidal and I went on our first date. He tells me to stop at the at nearest gas station and he fills my tank up. I thought at least he's not selfish and cheap. We stroll downtown in my car because his is falling apart and looks terrible. I took notice of all the kid fingerprints on the window and his car was full of what looked like junk. I told myself to keep in mind he is just a nice guy and we are just having adult fun.

He pays for dinner and we talked for hours. We did not want the night to end. I made it clear that I did not want to be in between him and ex-wife. It's not my style. I told him if he needed to work things out, that I am good. Vidal assured me it was time for him to move forward. He couldn't accomplish anything with her and he could no longer trust her. Vidal and I kept seeing each other, getting to know each other.

Vidal and I decided to make it exclusive when his divorce is final, but more red flags were starting to pop up. He had a picture of me in his car and his baby momma saw it. She started questioning him and saw me in the vehicle and drove off arrogantly. I'm thinking hasn't she moved on with her new boyfriend, what's the issue? Then she starts calling him late in the night. I told Vidal when a toxic woman knows you've moved on with someone else, she will sit on the sideline ready to cause drama. He didn't believe me at first, but the drama pursued anyway.

His ex was sending the kids to school smelling like cigarettes, getting them to school late, and not putting much

Things are getting serious between us, but before I go any further, I needed Vidal meet Grace.

thought in their wardrobe or hygiene. I suggested he should have a sit down with her. He did and she was better for a few weeks, but I told him to keep her accountable because this situation could get worse before it gets better. I knew if I wanted to be with this man, I would need him to handle his drama before it gets out of hand. I kept reminding myself that he is different, he is a kind and loving man.

My Husband

Less than six months of dating Vidal, he and I get married. Right after this, another red flag pops up, Vidal's mom Jesse. When we married his mom says, "why did he go and do that?"

I was hurt, felt like Girthy all over again. We moved past that topic fast; we were happy that's all that mattered. It was weird when Vidal said,

"I am your husband now. Let me hear you say it."

The words, "you are my husband," coming from my mouth sounded funny, but also really nice. Vidal did not have material things to offer but he had what I have always been searching for…unconditional LOVE. Like Beyonce said, "let me upgrade you," but we upgraded each other. We both were on a mission to get our lives together. Things were great between Vidal and me, my children even loved him. He took us on trips to different states, we went to church together, no worrying about money. Life was good! His children would come to visit and we did family things together and afterwards, they would return home to their mom. Vidal and I were happy, we both felt like life was giving us a break. He said he was tired of people pulling on him, I understood where he was coming from. He loved his family, but they were mentally draining him.

God Gave Me Red Flags
and I Was Warned

Our honeymoon stage ended fast. No one was happy their golden boy and ATM was no longer accessible to them. Vidal's children's mom, could not stand the fact we were happy. She definitely couldn't accept her children's father had moved on. She decides to move herself and the children out of Georgia in the middle of the school year without even telling him. Of course, he's stressed and worried, exactly what she wanted. I help him locate them and now she wins full custody of the children. I am always helping others so I am thinking why not help my husband in terms of helping raise these kids. I think, they're young, how bad can it be raising them. Ms. Tout warned me, reminding me how hard of a time I had with my own children. Our Black community has this stereotype that Black fathers are not there, but there are some who want to be there. I personally have seen a lot of Black women make it very difficult for them to be involved because the man no longer wants to be in a relationship with them.

Narcissistic & Toxic Women

Everything was moving faster; two years in our apartment and two years later, Vidal and I buy our first house. We worked together to build up his credit so we could purchase our first home. The haters were plotting though. Vidal had a new wife, new home, new car and new career. His ex-in-laws, baby momma, sister, and mom had their own mission.

I never heard the word, "narcissist," until I got involved with my husband. His baby momma and his former in-laws are narcissists. His sister and mother were also very nasty to me. All these women were jealous of our quick success and loving home. My husband mentioned one of his boys having some mental health issues and his family tried to use that against us to end our marriage. I helped him get full custody of his boys anyway and we didn't have to hire an attorney.

I should have thought this endeavor through more, although I was warned of what I was taking on. Vidal and I did not discuss what role I would play in his children's lives. Dealing with this family was toxic as hell, it brought me back to dealing with my own past. Jezebel was Jane number two. Vidal's former mother-in-law was like Josie in many ways. His mom, Jesse, was just like David's mom. His sister was sneaky and had her low-down ways. His boys were the "minis" of their mother and grandmother. They knew how to lie and manipulate quite well. The oldest, Jerome, was the ringleader. He reminded me of David. The only time they would listen to me was when they wanted something from me, like money or a ride from an activity.

When we were dating, Vidal would say I was not fully representing myself and we would laugh. As time went on and we're married, I realized he had not fully represented himself and his life. I told him he didn't tell me I would have to deal with such toxic women and all this stress. I simply had no more patience for these types of people. I've been dealing with abuse since the age of four. It's taken a toll on me and I shouldn't have to deal with this anymore. My youngest, Kentrell, said to me, "I thought you will be happy since you are married." At this point, I felt like a ticking time bomb. This is not what I imagined married life to be. It was supposed to be peaceful, and it was, until we got his children. It's harsh to say, but frankly, it's the truth.

His former in-laws and his family had one intention, which is cause problems in our home. Jerome receives a call from his grandmother. She asks him what we got him for his birthday and her response was, "that's all they got you." As a Black woman, you reading this, know these are harsh words. I told my husband he needs to check these people. They can't be telling a six-year-old that. What else could she be saying when he visits her. I was angry because her daughter didn't even give her own son anything on his birthday. Instead, she chose to move to Arkansas with her married boyfriend.

I told Vidal several times to address these toxic people. He did not and the situations got worst. They called the police to our place for a wellness check, like we are neglecting the children or something. I told his former mother-in-law if she would stop babying her daughter, then we could all parent these children properly. Or she can come get them. She believed nothing was wrong with her daughter's parenting skills or lack thereof. I lost all respect for her after that conversation.

I tried to remain calm, but eventually you just can't take anymore. I cursed his baby momma and her mother out. His children didn't want to listen to me, his baby momma is in and out of jail five times for not paying child support. His ex would call Vidal's job saying to call home to his wife. She would call his job to see if he was there, all I could think is his Crazy Baby Momma at it again.

I was thinking it was a mistake to get involved with this man. I would have never met another group of crazy and toxic people had I stayed away. Not all of us are GOD'S children, some are the devil's children.

After a few months of his children with us, I found out the oldest has a disorder called pica. I researched it and had never heard of this. People eat paper, furniture, carpet, etc. He has sickle cell as well. I am questioning Vidal about this because he failed to mention this information to me. My husband said he knew about the paper but did not know he would eat our carpet or other things. When Jezebel called the next time, I told her she gave her children these issues. They did

Before getting married, clean out your past and present issues. Do not bring problems to a new relationship or marriage. This saying that you also marry your spouse's family, is a lie. Genesis 2:24 Respect the relationship they have with their family if it is a healthy one.

not know how to properly hold silverware or simply eat at a dinner table. They didn't know how to bathe themselves; they would wet the bed as well.

I continue to be the good stepmother. I changed my schedule so I could help with homework and attend PTA meetings. My children are in middle school and college by this point. This interruption interfered with me developing a better relationship with my own children. My husband works late to provide and all these women are no help, just negativity.

I was overwhelmed. Vidal wasn't a lot of help. He was not ready to deal with his family issues at all. He leans on me a lot to help with his children. My compassion takes over and I am determined to teach the children right and not allow the four toxic women in their lives to ruin it. Vidal was a great person, husband, provider, and stepfather to my kids. I was determined to not allow anyone destroy our marriage or our vision. They could not stand our success and their personal lives were in shambles.

Rage in a Dark Place to Crashing

Trying to play nice with these people, I offered the first olive branch. I invited the family to several events at our home. These people never even offered me a glass of water. The first few years into our marriage, I visited the home where his sister, Precious, and mother, Jesse, lived. They had a picture of Vidal and his ex-wife and the children hanging up on the wall, pure evil. I got up to get some air. My husband followed. I was just so hurt.

This next issue topped them all. Vidal and I went to pay our respect at his grandmother's funeral. She was the kindest to me. The wake was being held at his aunt's house. As soon as we walk in, his mom didn't speak to me the whole time. I hadn't done anything to these people to deserve this kind of treatment. At the family reunion years later, his mom shows all kinds of photos of his ex-wife in the picture lineup.

Instead of trying to help raise the boys, these women would think of new ways to make it a living hell in our household. They would come up with lies and under mind our parenting capabilities. The children became too much for me to deal with. I was just tired. Tired of raising someone else's kids, who clearly didn't care about what I had to say anyway. Tired of cooking for them, cleaning up after them, tired of asking them to stop their shenanigans. Definitely tired of their crazy momma. I felt very unappreciated. I felt like I wasn't good enough. I was tired of people thinking I should shut my mouth and allow them to continue hurting me. I was tired of living in a dark place in which everyone wished me harm and thought I was their burnt trash.

Life was repeating itself. All of this reminds me of my children's dads and their crazy families.

I was trying to prove to people that could not care less that I am a good person. I was silently screaming for help trying to be a great mother, stepmother, and wife. Even my own mother thought this was a good time to further the abuse and pain I was already receiving. She would say some of the ugliest things to me and about my husband when I shared my feelings about everything going on. She would use my hurt feelings against me and find ways to make me feel even worse about myself.

This all made me not want his children around any longer. No one gave me credit or positive praise for all the work I was putting in. The hurtful words from my mom stung the most because it was coming from her. All my life I wanted her approval and to feel some love and support. Instead, she is blaming me for everyone else's screw ups.

I knew Vidal's ex-wife probably wanted him back although he did not want her. I mostly kept calm through it all. I wanted out of this marriage. I told Vidal we needed to live in separate places until your children move out. My husband had no issues with my children. I made sure I handled my past before entering our marriage. He never had to deal with baby daddy issues.

His children mom, Caron, tries to stir up issues as well. She fires up saying these are not my children, they are hers and Vidal's. I told her, "Bitch, you right. They aren't mine, come get them." This went on deaf ears. This drama should have never happened. I asked for a GOD- fearing man and GOD gave me this, but it came with a laundry list of tasks. The devil tried to break me, but it did not work. Instead, I am able to share my story to heal myself and in hopes to help others in similar situations.

It was so natural for my husband's children to lie and manipulate. They learned this from their mom and grandmother. Rage was building up in me. The little girl inside was screaming. I was in a dark place. I did not understand how these children could come from a nice man like my husband. I had to remember they were half of another set of DNA'S as well. I am grateful for my friend Grace. She told me,

"Del, you got a good man. Trust me, they have been using and mistreating your husband as well. You saved him from those monsters. Your anger stems from raising children all over again. You did your job raising your children already however."

At this point, I did not look at his children   *Psalms 3: 1-8* as such. They did their own damage just like adults. My heart felt for them because I knew what kind of mother they had, but at some point, you have to try to meet me in the middle. The least they could do is follow house rules. I am giving them my best while they are giving me their worst.

My experience with older Black women has been terrible overall, but there are a few that I will always hold dear to my heart. Ms. Emma, the woman who gave me great advice. Ms. Herrington, a daycare provider to my children and a shining light. Ms. Tout, a classy and sassy woman. She's the auntie that keeps it real and lets you know when you need to fix a situation. Finally, my dear friend of 30 years, Grace.

As I mentioned, this experience of being a stepmother brought back feelings of being an abused child and as a young mother in abusive relationships. Having my stepchildren in the home with me was like having Tom and David all over again. I felt like a child fighting for peace, fighting for a way out from the abusive lifestyle. I prayed to GOD,

"Please reveal the way I can get peace in my home. Please get rid of those who do not belong in my life. I am tired. I tried to be a good mom, stepmom, and wife, but I am slowly losing more of myself."

One of the few things easing my mind and stress was a dance class I managed to take. I lost some weight and I was happy. It was a long time since I had been that size, but that journey ended all too soon with the continued emotional stress.

I had to realize I would not be that successful at raising my stepchildren. The damage was already done way before they arrived to me. I could not help that much; it was like hitting my head on a brick wall trying to get through. Everyone was already waiting around and hoping I would fail. Dealing with narcissistic women is not easy. I kept telling myself, I am in it to win it. I will not let them get the best of me and my household. Inside, I felt like I was dying and I kept asking, how long can I continue to take this.

Situations happened that brought us to homeschooling his kids. It was even more toxic drama from Vidal's family. Ms. Tout knew I had a plan, but she also knew I didn't need to be bothered with this anymore. She was right. My plan was to get the kids graduated from high school and send them on their way to their grandmother. I knew I would not feel peace until I got them out of my house and stopped dealing with his family. Their mom started coming back into their lives when they turned 18. I thought, of course, after I did the hard part of raising them. I enrolled them in college and the younger one, Bobby, did attend for a while but Jerome did not. They did not have much encouragement from their mom or grandma. They left and started working in fast food restaurants to help support their mom and grandma.

I do care about the boys despite what others think. It was just incredibly difficult having to raise them and deal with their family. Through all that drama, Vidal and I still enjoyed each other. GOD answered my calling and restored peace to my home. Nobody can tell me GOD is not real. Vidal and I fought for our marriage and I fought for my peace of mind. At the end of the day, my husband needs me just as much as I need him. We have been married for 15 years now. The devil thought he was going to break us, but can't nobody separate what GOD has ordained. I blame no one, I forgive everyone, and I hope others will forgive me as nothing negative was done intentionally.

Ex Daughter-in-Law and Her Mother

I know life has its challenges. We get upset when life brings sad situations to us. But, no one could have prepared me for how sick in the head my former daughter-in-law, Ester, and her mother, Shanna, are. The lies they told government authorities, could have damaged our life. My oldest, KJ, experienced the abuse right along with me when he was a child. He sees my trauma and unfortunately, he marries into a family with similar issues. Again, GOD gives us regular red flags to look out for going into a relationship and there were plenty with his ex-wife. My son similar marriage becomes a repeat drama with Black women.

I am to the point of wondering what is with Black women.

GOD has fought all of my battles and protected me from so much harm. I am eternally grateful for his mercy and love over my life. This little black girl is not your burnt black trash.

Memories of My Grandmother Daisy

When my grandmother, Daisy Jones, passed away, I was clinging to my mother. Wherever she went, I was there at her hip. It was devastating losing my stepfather, then Victor, and now my grandmother. I felt like everyone I loved was leaving me. Sometimes, when alone, I would sit on the floor and just cry. I spent time with my grandmother over the years and I was a companion to her. I would sit with her, while my cousin Charles was out back with his friends. I used to be scared she would die on me. When she would nod off into a nap, I would say, "grandma you okay? You awake? You need something or me to call someone?"

My grandma would reply with, "shit, I'm sleep." And we both would laugh. I used to help my grandmother wrap her foot after the doctor cut it off, but left a bone sticking out. We would go shopping together and this was always funny. When I started driving, the deal was in order to drive my mom's car after school, I had to go sit and help my grandmother get around. Eventually she had another foot amputated. One time when we were at a retail store, one of my contacts fell out. I asked her to help me find it and she said, "shit I can't see either." My grandmother was hilarious. She would teach

KJ to say the word, "shit." I would tell her don't teach my baby to curse, but she thought it was funny. My grandmother been through a lot, I watched her cry for her son. It hurts me so much to know whenever she was hurt.

I truly miss my grandmother, but she is with me in spirit. Anytime I go through anything difficult, *I feel her comfort* She showed up a lot during the toxic years with my husband's family.

I Can Breathe, this is Me

Money and material things do not give you peace. I fought so hard for my peace; I was living through life in survival mode. I thank GOD every day for keeping me and allowing me to enjoy my children through the survival. I am smelling the roses more, like I always wanted in life. When I lived and worked in the suburbs of Atlanta, in the Buckhead community; I saw only white women strolling with their children at the park in the morning and afternoon. I used to say that I want that. I was fortunate to have to work weekends or late hours most of my children's childhoods. I prayed to GOD to give me the opportunity to take my children to school and drop them off daily. HE gave me just that. It meant a lot to me and my children. I wanted to have some sense of balance, to be hands on as much as possible with my children. I must give myself credit, it was not easy, but I did not pass up opportunities to learn and grow.

I can breathe so much better, see so much clearer. I am doing more of what I always loved doing, which is volunteering in my community. The volunteer opportunities I enjoy is cutting grass, volunteering at the Hosea Feed the Hunger, and being a Girl Scouts Leader. I mentored at an elementary school, volunteered for a church cleaning. I always picked up trash in every community I lived in. Keeping a clean environment is important to me.

I created two businesses for myself. A license learning home daycare and a lawn service. I have the time to do my dance classes, I never stop my walks, and our backyard is decorated to be a place of nature and serenity. My alone time is my everything. I enjoy skating and going to the park with my granddaughters. I do my best to keep my peace. Yes, there's still people around who hate to see me happy, for me, I do my best to not give them my energy.

You have your health; you can accomplish anything. Times will get hard, but you must keep going. Find your inner peace and enjoy the simple things in life.

I keep in my mind it is not my responsibility to make anyone happy. People have a responsibility to not over burden others with their life journey, however. Things will happen that's out of our control and things will happen that are completely in our control. I ask myself now, is it worth arguing or fighting with the person(s).

Our marriage is stronger, my husband and I feel more like we are living for GOD and us and not for others.

Looking for a mother

Looking for a mother, in search of a mother's special love. I look at other girl's relationship with their mother. I yearn for that bond. I look at girl's fashion styles, did they learn that from their mother?

Hugs, kisses, and hearing the words I love you from a mother.

I never felt that mother and daughter magic. I heard from sister and stepsister the love they received from our mother. This I rarely got. I look for this emotional bond from other older women that look like me.

I know I am all grown up, but the little girl in me still wanted the feeling of a mother's love. I had to accept the love my mother gave me is all she is willing to give. I will always love and cherish my mother. I no longer look for mother to support and comfort me. I am my own unique woman, who has been anointed by GOD to be her own woman, so, I am no longer looking for a mother.

My Dad, I love You R.I.P
Army Veteran

My dad returns in my life on two occasions to live with me. When I got first apartment in Georgia and when I delivered my child. He meets both David and Tom. He saw David throw a tantrum, my dad said, "you need to get rid of him before he kills you, then I'll have him killed."

My dad here with me was good for my children. They were able to spend great time with their grandfather. My dad brought my daughter her first black baby doll. When he came to live with me again, it was when he was waiting for his apartment to get ready in Georgia. He did watch my children with Ms. Tout while I was at the hospital giving birth.

My dad too cannot go without hurting my self-esteem. In the hospital, with my third child, he says to me, "you need to lose weight." That was very hurtful.

My dad returns in 2017 to live in Georgia. It was so nice having him here. He gave me another bike, the same color as the one when I was 13. I thank him for getting me started in the lawn business. For most of his life, my dad worked for himself. I got my entrepreneurship skills from him. On multiple occasions he did try to be nasty and mean to me. Every time, I turned it into something positive. I would tell him I loved him and there was nothing he could do about it. That I was not going to fight with him and that I wanted a positive relationship with him.

We moved on to a positive relationship. He would go fishing and bring back some for me. He would even take me out to breakfast. We gave him his last birthday party at 70 years old. He looked happy, we danced and exchanged heartful words. I am so glad I kept it peaceful. I saw my dad for the last time on March 25, 2020 before he went to the hospital. April 23, 2020, he passed away.

After he passed, he visited me in my dreams. He says, "I do not believe in death, I am not dead."

My dad was not there like I would have liked him to be, but I appreciate him for putting in the effort when he was around. He was a good grandfather to my children, and I appreciate that. Anytime my children needed something, he was there. He paid for the catering at KJ's wedding.

My dad like me always wanted to feel loved and accepted by his mother and his family. Like me, he would give his money and time to everyone that would love us and want us around. His final day, we laid him to rest peacefully. It's sad to see my father do much for so many and receive so little. I was so disheartened.

*I shared this information on
behalf of my late father*

*YHWH gave the world laws and
commandments not religions.
Letter J was invented the year 1524
Revelation 1:14-15*

Letter

Dear Black Women,

I forgive you. We are all dealing with something. The world has told us we are not beautiful and that we are not enough. The world has mistreated us, told us we do not matter. They enslaved our ancestors with the intent to destroy our self-worth. They have pitted us against each other. Our Black men have not done enough to protect us. They too have been abused by this world, but we all have a responsibility to uplift each other. We have a responsibility to expect more from our sons and nurture both our sons and daughters.

We have a responsibility to demand more from our men when we are in relationships with them. We have a responsibility in our communities, to make the environment better. We must teach other and learn from each other. We have a responsibility to carry ourselves with self-respect and to never accept anything less than respect. We do not have to destroy our fellow sister's character to get ahead in life. Yes, you cannot help everyone. You cannot save everyone. Everyone may not want help, but ask yourself, have you lent a helping hand to your Sista?

I am aware many of us were not taught how to be a wife. I can share what it is not. It's not keeping a nasty house, a nasty car, etc. It's not allowing children to go unattended. It's not gossiping on the phone with your girlfriends when your husband is home. It's not inviting women friends to your home when your husband is home. It's not allowing your husband to be the handy man to your women neighbors, family, and friends. It's not keeping yourself physically, mentally, spiritually, and emotionally unwell.

I fell in this behavior of being a baby mother before marriage. Save yourself for the right one. You will be glad you did. Don't fall in the trap of a marriage that does not work. It often does work when both of you clean your dirty laundry before saying, "I do," and always keeping GOD first in everything you do. HE will protect you and your spouse through the storms.

I say to you, never get a man who does not know GOD. Remember, you must know GOD as well. We all mess up. One thing I know about serving HIM, he wants us to simply do our best and give our best to HIM. Live according to HIS will and not the false narrative this world is teaching.

Being a wife comes with learning your spouse, praying over them, praying together, and not putting them before GOD. Keep your personal business inside your home. If it's not putting you in harm's way, almost everything is a give and take. It's effective communication. It's learning how to listen to each other. Disagreement will arise, but it's about never going to bed mad. It's not getting burnt out. It is keeping a clean and organized home so each of you can think clearly. It's getting up early and having you time to get your mind right for the day. It's finding some alone time. It's keeping it fun, spending time together without the family or children. It's not allowing your husband to lack in his duties.

Lastly, let's throw away the negative stories the world has put upon us. They do not belong to us, so throw them back.

Remember you are beautiful, made in HIS image. Take your time to know yourself. Heal from your past. It is okay to slip up, to cry, feel overwhelmed, angry, etc. You are human. Now go out and be the queen you are.

THIS LITTLE BLACK GIRL
AIN'T YOUR BURNT TRASH

The world did not give you this joy therefore the world cannot take it away.

People in the world will make it a mission to destroy you. Will gather and wish you harm, spread false lies, intentionally set out to harm you...but oh my...the heavenly father will always protect his anointed. They cannot break what they did not build, you are a child of the Most-High.

Little Black girl you are beautifully made from your hair, to your toes. Be yourself, and keep the creator of the earth first at all times.